P9-CBQ-769

Praise for

UNITED BREAKS GUITARS

"Dave Carroll tells the inspiring tale of how he handled a frustrating situation nonconfrontationally, with a mission of 'improving the world, one experience at a time.' His story resonated with me, and it will move you, too!"

— **Dr. Wayne W. Dyer,** #1 *New York Times* best-selling author of *Wishes Fulfilled* and *Excuses Begone*!

"This may be one of the most humble stories ever told by a man who changed the world."

— **Josh Bernoff,** co-author of *Groundswell*

"Dave Carroll's 'United Breaks Guitars' is a brilliant use of social media, and Taylor Guitars jumped on that idea quickly, simply, and honestly, following Dave's lead. The exposure we gained from the message, well placed, was essentially free and had a very positive effect on our brand and our business. It's easy to believe that one could not possibly afford to buy that kind of exposure, as we experienced the power of social media."

— **Bob Taylor,** co-founder and president of Taylor Guitars

"As anyone who's heard him sing or seen him speak knows, Dave Carroll is a master storyteller. In this delightful and insightful book, Dave unveils the amazing true story of the video sensation that changed the worlds of social media and customer service."

— **David Rogers,** author of *The Network Is Your Customer*

"The story of Dave Carroll's broken guitar is the profoundly moving account of how one man took on an implacable system and won. In a world pervaded by doom and gloom, his story is a rare and welcome burst of sunshine."

— **Frank McKenna,** former Premier of New Brunswick and former Canadian Ambassador to the United States

"If you have customers, then you should read this book to understand how one frustrated—and talented—customer named Dave Carroll taught corporate America how to treat people better."

— **Charlene Li,** author of *Open Leadership* and co-author of *Groundswell*

"By far, the greatest story of one person's social-media victory over big-airline lies and mistreatment. It's why all companies better stand up and pay attention to every single voice. You will love Dave Carroll, his story, his victory, and his YouTube video. This is not just a book. It's a service lesson and a warning about social consumerism."

— **Jeffrey Gitomer**, author of *Customer Satisfaction Is Worthless, Customer Loyalty Is Priceless*

"Dave Carroll has become the poster child for the potential of social media as a catalyst for transformational and organizational change. 'United Breaks Guitars' demonstrates the power of one individual to make a difference and stand up for his or her rights as a customer. Smart companies would do exceptionally well to listen, learn, and make sure this never happens to them . . . or if it does, make sure they're equipped to respond properly. And as for United, I haven't flown with them since . . ."

— **Joseph Jaffe**, author of *Flip the Funnel*

"We live in a global village—one in which everyone is interconnected. Dave Carroll's amazing story reminds us of the promise and peril of that connection. Always the poignant wordsmith, his message provides a powerful wake-up call that should jolt us into assuming responsibility while demonstrating respect!"

— **Chip R. Bell**, co-author of *Wired and Dangerous*

"Dave Carroll is a certified music and social-media superstar. His spectacular 'Dave' vs. Goliath 'United Breaks Guitars' video shows that even one individual can outgun one of the largest, most scientific marketing, PR, and customer-service organizations on the planet. For individuals and organizations to get noticed today, it takes speed and agility, plus the kind of creative imagination and craft skill that allowed Dave to write a song every bit as powerful as a Stinger missile."

— **David Meerman Scott**, author of *The New Rules of Marketing and PR* and co-author of *Marketing Lessons from the Grateful Dead*

"This story has captured the attention of the world with regard to the power of one person with a social-media platform. Executives should read this story and heed its warnings, and consumers will be uplifted by the voice that Dave Carroll has given them."

— **Dr. Catriona Wallace**, director of Fifth Quadrant, Sydney, Australia

UNITED BREAKS GUITARS

ALSO BY DAVE CARROLL

CD Recordings

Raincoat in Vegas (Dave Carroll)

Perfect Blue (Dave Carroll)

Instant Christmas (Sons of Maxwell)

Sunday Morning (Sons of Maxwell)

Among the Living (Sons of Maxwell)

Sailors Story (Sons of Maxwell)

Live at Tim's House (Sons of Maxwell)

The Neighbourhood (Sons of Maxwell)

Bold Frontier (Sons of Maxwell)

Sons of Maxwell (Sons of Maxwell)

UNITED BREAKS GUITARS

THE POWER OF ONE VOICE IN THE AGE OF SOCIAL MEDIA

DAVE CARROLL

HAY HOUSE, INC.
Carlsbad, California • New York City
London • Sydney • Johannesburg
Vancouver • Hong Kong • New Delhi

Published and distributed in the United States by: Hay House, Inc.: www.hayhouse.com® • ***Published and distributed in Australia by:*** Hay House Australia Pty. Ltd.: www.hayhouse.com.au • ***Published and distributed in the United Kingdom by:*** Hay House UK, Ltd.: www.hayhouse.co.uk • ***Published and distributed in the Republic of South Africa by:*** Hay House SA (Pty), Ltd.: www.hayhouse.co.za • ***Distributed in Canada by:*** Raincoast: www.raincoast.com • ***Published in India by:*** Hay House Publishers India: www.hayhouse.co.in

Project editor: Alex Freemon
Cover design: Amy Rose Grigoriou • *Interior design:* Pamela Homan

Library of Congress Cataloging-in-Publication Data

Carroll, Dave.
United breaks guitars : the power of one voice in the age of social media / Dave Carroll.
p. cm.
ISBN 978-1-4019-3793-5 (hbk. : alk. paper)
1. Carroll, Dave 2. United Airlines--Public relations--Case studies. 3. Consumer complaints--Case studies. 4. Customer relations--Case studies. 5. Internet videos--Social aspects--Case studies. 6. Social media--Case studies. I. Title.
HF5415.52.C37 2012
658.8'12--dc23

2011051468

Hardcover ISBN: 978-1-4019-3793-5
Digital ISBN: 978-1-4019-3795-9

15 14 13 12 4 3 2 1
1st edition, May 2012

Printed in the United States of America

To my son, Flynn,
for the difference you have already made.
My wish is that this book will
remind you of your own
unlimited potential.

Love, Dad

CONTENTS

FOREWORD

In March 2008, Dave Carroll stepped onto a United Airlines plane from Halifax to Chicago and changed the world.

Dave is the iconic creator of "United Breaks Guitars," an impassioned video ballad that describes his months-long trek through the world of airline customer service, illustrated with mariachi singers, catchy country-style music, and clever visuals. But "United Breaks Guitars" is far more than music. With more than 11.5 million views, it's a highly visible marker that business has changed forever, and that customers have taken over. This is truly the age of the customer, because any customer can, in theory, do what Dave Carroll did: use talent, fight back, connect with millions of other customers, and knock hundreds of millions of dollars off the market value of a massive corporation.

This engaging book tells Dave's story from the inside. As you'll learn, he's one of the nicest guys on the planet, just a musician trying to do a great job. Despite the way he was treated, Dave shares the almost loving way he tweaked United after trying every other imaginable strategy. This may be one of the most humble stories ever told by a man who changed the world. You'll read about Dave's upbringing and the family life that shaped him, his struggles as a musician, and how he's taken this experience and used it, not only to build his career, but to give back to the people who helped him along the way, and to support the causes—such as first responders and local-news coverage—that he feels strongly about.

Embedded in this story are also nuggets of insight for anyone in a business, large or small. If you're wondering what social technology means to your company, take a close look at what it meant to the companies Dave talks about in this story—not just United Airlines but Taylor Guitars, Ford, and Chubb insurance. These companies have been changed by social technology—United now uses "United Breaks Guitars" in its customer-service training, for example. They understand that social sites like YouTube and Facebook represent not just a threat from unhappy customers, but a unique way to listen and engage with all customers, improve your products, and improve your company's image.

As a business author, these elements are my stock-in-trade—case studies and strategy frameworks. But Dave's experience frames these ideas in a wholly personal way. In hundreds of stories and interviews, from CNN to *The View,* Dave's story has become familiar to many of us, but inside it is an uplifting tale of how you can change the world with a smile and a guitar. As you read about Dave's personal journey from musician to video star to activist to social-media expert and public speaker, I hope you think, *Hey, I could do something like that.* Because in the totally connected world of social technologies, each of us now has the potential to change the world.

—**Josh Bernoff**
Best-selling co-author of *Groundswell:*
Winning in a World Transformed by Social Technologies

♬ ♪ ♬ ♪ ♬

Part I

SETTING THE STAGE

Chapter 1

AND SO IT BEGAN

"Congratulations, Dave. Your 'United Breaks Guitars' video is widely lauded as one of the most important in Google's history!"

That was the beginning of an e-mail I received from a Google employee nearly one year after posting my first YouTube music video, about a less-than-stellar experience with United Airlines. Given the billions of videos hosted on YouTube since its inception, that e-mail suggested to me that my $150 music-video project had literally become a one-in-a-billion experience!

The foundation of my story is in no way unique. I went through what anyone who has ever flown commercially has gone through: a bad customer-service experience with an airline. Today, though, anyone can share their story directly with a mass audience, and using social media, I shared mine in the best way I knew how: with a song and a music video called "United Breaks Guitars."

On July 6, 2009, I was maintaining a successful career as a completely independent musician and singer-songwriter from Halifax, Canada. I had no manager, agent, publicist, record label, or distributor for my recordings. In addition to managing my own first solo CD recording in 2008, I had been totally self-contained for 20 years in a duo called Sons of Maxwell with my brother, Don.

On July 7, 2009, I was still all of those things, but change was on the way. The night before, I had uploaded my first music video to YouTube. People began tuning in and sharing my four-minute creation. Today, if you consider the total audience of the traditional and online media that covered my story, that video has reached more than 150 million people across the world, and it launched me into the midst of a full-scale media frenzy.

The ripples made by this simple and campy video have traveled from boardrooms to classrooms, and to anywhere an Internet connection can be found. It has established a benchmark within customer service for years to come and became a shining example of the power of social media.

In the year that followed the video's launch, my story was told in the world's leading newspapers and daily news programs. It was featured on BBC, CNN, and all major U.S. broadcast networks. I've appeared on ABC's *The View* and on Oprah Radio, and I've been featured in *The New York Times, Rolling Stone* magazine, and *Reader's Digest.* The Harvard Business School has done a case study on "United Breaks Guitars," and dozens of books on customer service and social media include references to my experience to give context to their theses.

In September 2009, if you did a Google search of "United Breaks Guitars," you'd have pulled up over 20 million references online. This story has gone wide and deep. In July of that year, I had the number one most-watched YouTube music video in the world and the number six most-watched YouTube video of any kind. Yet like so many powerful things, it began with a simple idea.

ALTHOUGH THE VIDEO WAS LAUNCHED on July 6, 2009, the story behind "United Breaks Guitars" was born much earlier, during an airline trip from Halifax to Omaha on March 31, 2008. Sons of Maxwell had been hired to do a five-stop tour of Nebraska by the arts presenter for the state, the University of Nebraska.

To get there, we booked four flights with United Airlines, starting from Halifax and with a scheduled connection at O'Hare Airport in Chicago. If this is starting to sound a little like the theme song to *Gilligan's Island,* it may be because the result is so similar. What should have been a routine business trip became a comedy of errors the likes of which far too many people continue to experience each day.

The band and I started our trip at Halifax Stanfield International Airport and checked in at the United Airlines counter. I was traveling with Don, bass player Mike Hiltz, and electric-guitar player Jon Park-Wheeler. I recall asking the agent at check-in if I could carry my guitars with me into the cabin and being told no.

I had never flown United before, but Canada's largest airline, Air Canada, has enforced a policy of checking musical instruments for as long as I can remember, so I didn't argue with the United agent who denied my request. I remember that I wasn't asked to sign a damage waiver for my guitars upon check-in. Many airlines compel musicians to sign a waiver that releases the airline from any liability should their instruments be destroyed in transit. United has that policy, but as I've experienced with different carriers, it is not always enforced by their agents.

When musicians fly, they bring their luggage and their instruments—except drummers, who fly "luggage only," since they are averse to resembling pack mules when they travel. While drum kits, guitar amps, microphones, and other essential musical devices can be rented at almost any destination, for the most part, a musician's instrument is a one-of-a-kind tool that often becomes an expression of him or her. Think of Willie Nelson and it's difficult to imagine him playing anything other than that old beat-up nylon-string guitar.

For this tour, I had wisely decided to bring two guitars with me to hedge against unforeseen circumstances. We didn't have the budget on this trip to travel with a road manager, sound engineer, or instrument technician, so I wore those hats as well. If something such as a string breaking were to occur onstage, we had to be prepared to manage that in real time by easily making the switch on the fly.

The two guitars I brought were both valued high-end instruments that I had owned for quite some time. One was an Ovation Elite, and the other a Taylor 710ce. It was the latter that would end up being the focus of all the attention in this story.

The flight to Chicago was uneventful. But then upon landing, a woman sitting one row behind me and across the aisle looked to the tarmac and said words that would make any musician cringe: "Oh my God, they're throwing guitars out there." I snapped to attention and asked her to repeat herself. When she did, it sounded just as horrible the second time.

Mike, who was in the window seat just in front of this woman, looked out to see the handlers chucking his bass guitar some amount of distance from the belt to the luggage cart. I actually never saw the guitars being thrown myself, but there must have been sufficient loft and distance for an objective observer to feel compelled to say so out loud.

As band leader, I decided to wait for everyone to deplane before alerting the flight attendant. When I met her in the aisle and began to share the story, she literally raised her hand in front of my face and said, "Don't talk to me; talk to the lead agent." I asked her where I might find such a person. She said she was just outside the plane on the ramp to the terminal.

When I exited the aircraft, the only person on the ramp was a United employee who was quickly walking away. I called out, "Excuse me, I was told that I should speak to the lead agent about the way our instruments were being handled on the tarmac." She didn't miss a step and replied curtly over her shoulder, "I'm not the lead agent," and escaped into the bustling crowd at O'Hare.

Beginning to see a pattern, I immediately sought out a United employee in the terminal at our arrival gate. She was preparing to board her next flight, so for the third time, I tried to explain what had been seen from the cabin. Before picking up the phone to make a call, she tilted her head to the side and said in a soft, patronizing voice, "Yeah, but hon, that's why you signed the waiver." I had been rejected by three women in less than five minutes. Not since that time in college had I experienced that kind of rejection!

None of the three women disputed what had happened, and that trio of short responses spoke volumes. I got the message: "This stuff happens all the time, no one cares, we won't be doing anything about it, and you should just accept it."

I interjected and began trying to explain that I hadn't signed the waiver and that no waiver I'll ever recognize makes throwing instruments acceptable, but she had already started speaking to another person on the phone.

Having been dismissed and needing to find my connection, I walked away flustered, bewildered, and hoping that the cases carrying our guitars were tough enough to withstand the handling they'd received.

Our plane to Omaha was late departing Chicago (something I was told to expect at this busy airport), so we arrived in Nebraska after midnight. I remember we were all pretty tired and eager to check in to the airport hotel quickly, because our driver from Lincoln was coming to collect us at around 6 A.M.

When we retrieved our luggage, there were no United employees within sight at the baggage belt. I've since been told that they must have been nearby, but my experience supports the theory that maybe they had just gotten tired and went home early. Either way, they weren't present to talk to at the belt.

My Ovation case looked fine, and the Taylor one felt intact to the touch. The cases from the Taylor factory are above-average hard-shell cases. They feel more solid and weigh more because they protect the instrument better than a standard hard-shell case. To lengthen the life of the Taylor case and protect it against nicks and tears,

I had bought a soft, padded nylon case with one-inch foam that fits over the factory case. Essentially this was a case for my case. I had it designed to fit like a glove, so it takes some work to get it off.

Having flown with this guitar dozens of times without incident, I felt the body of the case for any dents or damage, and at 12:30 A.M., we determined that we should just go to the hotel and sleep. At this point, I believed and hoped that our guitars had been simply mishandled and not broken.

The next morning our van arrived, and we drove a few hours to our first tour stop and got ready for sound check. It was then that I pulled out my Taylor, only to discover that it was badly damaged. There was a four-inch opening in the base at the tail block (the place where you would plug in your guitar cable). Not only that, but the cedar-top body was cracked in long, almost parallel lines and had separated from the sidewalls of the guitar. My guess is that it had been thrown and landed on its tailpin with the neck pointing straight up. In any case, I was about to start a road trip with my favorite guitar smashed. I decided my only option was to put the Taylor back in its case and not look at it again until I returned to Omaha, and I was grateful I had my Ovation to complete the tour. Aside from this, the tour went off without a hitch, and we enjoyed enthusiastic audiences at all venues.

But I knew I would need to present the Taylor guitar to a United employee to open a claim. Since I had no plans to be near an airport for the next week, I decided to wait until I began my return trip to do so. Upon check-in in Omaha, I started telling United's staff what had happened and moved to show the damage to the agent when I was stopped and told that she didn't need to see it. She said I would have to show the damage and open a claim at the airport where my trip began, back in Halifax.

When I got back to Canada, I was told that United had no official presence in Halifax. And so it continued! Yes, I had flown in a plane that had UNITED painted on the side and been checked in by people wearing United uniforms, but it was Air Canada, United's Star Alliance partner, who is the company's point of contact in Halifax. Now I got the story from Air Canada's baggage representative that the best they could do was offer me a blue United pamphlet with a toll-free number on it. I was told I would need to call that number to open the claim.

CALL IT INTUITION, BUT I ABSOLUTELY KNEW that I was at the start of what would be a very long process, so I made two vows to myself that day: first, I would not give up until this matter was resolved to my satisfaction; and second, I would never lose my temper in any of my interactions. I would do my best to be respectful to everyone I encountered, knowing that they were simply trying to do their jobs within the rules they were given.

I went home, and the next day I called the toll-free number, which connected me with a call center in India. They suggested I bring the guitar in to O'Hare for inspection. I explained that I lived in another city, a different time zone, and another country. After much confusion, I was told to go back to the Halifax airport to open the claim and have the damage inspected there. I returned to Stanfield International Airport the next day, and despite Air Canada's protest that this was not their responsibility, they opened a claim number, inspected the damage, and rejected the claim from an Air Canada perspective. Why should Air Canada pay for damage caused on a United flight by United baggage handlers? That would make for a dandy partnership if United could manage it, but it's not realistic. I was told that the "rejection" would remove Air Canada's liability, but the claim number would get me started with United and establish that the damage I was claiming actually existed.

Meanwhile, I had the guitar inspected by a respected technician and was informed that it was irreparable. The tail block is an essential part of a guitar, and I was told that mine was cracked. The repair tech didn't feel he could fix it, but I thought it might be worth getting a second opinion. About a month later, I contacted Harland Suttis. He had decades of experience repairing guitars, was Taylor certified, and lived near Halifax.

I shipped the guitar to Harland, and he had it for months before sending it back to me with a beautiful repair. It looked and sounded great when played acoustically—but I found that onstage and plugged into a sound system, it had lost some of its magic, so I decided to retire the instrument from active service. Still, I was thrilled to have it back, and although I don't tour with it anymore, I play it almost daily for my own enjoyment. The price of that repair was $1,200. So now I had an exact cost of the damage caused . . . for all the good it would end up doing me.

♫ ♪ ♫ ♪ ♫

Chapter 2

THE BOND BETWEEN A MAN AND HIS GUITAR

At this point, before we go any further, you need to understand something. You need to know that a guitar player's instrument is never just luggage. It's important to understand that when we buy our instruments, the process is not unlike a courtship, and when musicians commit to a guitar, many times we marry these instruments for life! We may be accused of polygamy, but that's the way it is. I personally own eight guitars from various eras in my life; like so many musicians, I simply have trouble saying good-bye to any of my instruments.

With so many makes and models these days, a guitar is a hugely personal choice, and most musicians invest significant time researching and testing countless models before buying theirs. As in life, different personalities initiate romance with their own unique style, and I'd like to share with you my process that eventually led to meeting my Taylor 710ce so many years ago.

When buying a guitar, I enter the store like Clint Eastwood walking into a strange saloon, pausing just inside the entryway with doors still swinging, scanning the room with eyes only, face forward. For added drama, I enter with the theme to *The Good, the Bad and the Ugly* playing on my iPod.

When I zero in on the acoustic-guitar section, I move toward it, but I take the long way getting there, not wanting to appear desperate and alert the guitars to the fact that "I'm interested." I walk slowly but with confidence, and at first, I walk right past them, pretending not to notice the parade of finely polished wood and steel.

You see, I'm doing the walk-by test. It's a very important first test, and it's during the walk-by that you wait for one of the guitars to catch your eye and speak to you. While some players make a beeline for the entry-level guitar racks, listening for a quick and dirty message that equates to "Hey, sailor, buy me a drink," I move directly to the high-end section.

I'm looking for a long-term relationship here, and as I walk past these finely crafted instruments, I'm listening for one to say, "Oh, excuse me. You look like an old friend. Do we know each other, and might we enjoy a rumba?"

If that happens, I stop. I turn slowly and deliberately with a confident grin and give the guitar a thorough visual exam beginning at the headstock to learn its name. My eyes drop down to its neck, then to the body and back to the top. It's a look that says, "I don't believe we've met, but hello, my name's Dave. May I play you?" By this time, Barry White appears on my iPod.

From there we move to the feel-test that requires a stool, and one can always be found near the high-end guitar area. Out of respect, the first order of business is to take off your jacket and lay it on the dirty floor. Zippers and metal buttons pose a danger to the finish of a fine instrument, so respectful guitar shoppers don't worry that there isn't a hook for their coat. The most seasoned shoppers simply wear fleece (and possibly even angora if you have the self-confidence to pull it off).

It's how a guitar feels in your grasp that you notice first. Does your body fit the guitar's body? Guitars come in different shapes and sizes, and sometimes they just don't feel right. Big people may not feel comfortable playing a small parlor-size instrument, just as diminutive folks are unlikely to buy a model that contains the word *Jumbo* in its name. It does happen, but we're not here to judge. It's simply a matter of taste.

Once in your arms, it has to sound right, and what comes next is not unlike a magical first kiss. Either it's there or it isn't, and with the first-kiss test, you know in that one strum if the tone has what you're looking for or not. Does playing feel easier on this instrument? Does it make you want to play more? Do you find yourself thinking, *I can't believe my fingers are making these beautiful sounds and I'm not even trying*? If that isn't happening, you politely put the guitar back with a mumbled apology, and suggest that you just be good friends. Then you walk away. It's best to end it quickly, rather than force something that will just never be.

If the guitar has passed all the tests, however, and you get to this point, you're hooked! If you're like most professional musicians, it's now that you look at the price . . . for the first time. You gasp! You blanch! Your eyes well up with tears, and with a crackling voice you look back at the guitar and say, "But baby, I love you. Don't worry. I'll make this work . . . somehow we'll be together."

You compose yourself and lay the guitar back on its hook carefully. If no one's looking, you might stroke its neck one time, and even kiss it. You retrieve your coat from the dirty floor and walk away, but not before sparing a parting glance for your new love and jealously scanning the store for anyone showing remote interest in her. That night you dream about her, and the next day, you return to the store to make the purchase, either having pawned a family heirloom you stole from your parents' house or you negotiate a financing option at loan-shark interest rates.

I purchased my Taylor 710ce in 1999 for $3,500 in much this fashion (using something closer to the financing option). It's a beautiful cedar-top acoustic guitar with a cutaway body and great tone. It stood out to me in the store over all others, and my 710 was present for the writing of some of my favorite songs, inspired by some of my most important life experiences. It's also the instrument I chose to play when crystallizing my music in the recording studio.

It's a fact that most professional musicians eke out a living near or below the poverty line. If we don't carry our instrument on board our flights, it's likely because the airlines refuse to allow us to, and we simply can't afford to buy an extra seat for it in the cabin. It also serves to explain why, when my guitar was mishandled and damaged, I refused to let United Airlines off the hook.

Now that we've established what an instrument means to its owner, I can get on with the frustrating story that led to the making of "United Breaks Guitars."

♫ ♪ ♫ ♪ ♫

Chapter 3

THE CUSTOMER-SERVICE DANCE WITH MS. IRLWEG

After I returned from my trip and opened a damage claim in Halifax, my experience proceeded to get increasingly complicated and confusing. I introduced myself to several United baggage and customer-service departments and was sent on more than my fair share of wild-goose chases.

I felt like the protagonist in a Dr. Seuss book, being sent "here, there, and everywhere," and encountering strange and wonderful characters along the way. The people in India, although sincere in their apologies and as helpful as they were empowered to be, could never seem to find the claim number opened by Air Canada until they were just about to give up. I would be directed to what I was told would be a solution, only to be rerouted back to India to start over again.

At one point, I was directed to an O'Hare baggage department and armed with a phone number. Someone eventually called me back and invited me to bring the guitar to . . . Chicago! Realizing that was impossible, they did the next logical thing and gave me the number of central baggage in New York, where I was told they would be able to process the claim. When I called that number, the person's first question was, "How did you get this number?"

I was shocked when she actually expressed interest in helping me by asking me to fax her all my information and to call back in a few days. I did that and phoned her one week later. She didn't remember who I was and said that the information never arrived. I implored her to look again, and when she did, she discovered my fax on what I imagined to be a cluttered desk full of unanswered correspondence.

She said that with the information now in her hands, she would need a couple of days to digest it. I called back a few days later only to discover that this secret number to central baggage in New York, which had apparently been compromised by me, had been disconnected, and I was rerouted to . . . India again!

This went on for *seven months*—from the first week of April until November 2008—until I finally received an e-mail from a customer-service representative in Chicago named Ms. Irlweg (rhymes with "twirl-whig"). Her first name was noted in her e-mail, but since she addressed me as Mr. Carroll, I returned the courtesy, and she has since been, and always will be, Ms. Irlweg to me.

I was thrilled to actually have contact with a real decision maker, and Ms. Irlweg and I exchanged a series of polite e-mails where I would outline my case and she would rebut each point as to why the airline would not be held accountable for any damages. It became "our thing," and Ms. Irlweg was a seasoned pro!

Each time I wrote, I approached my claim from different angles, and every time, she was polite and direct and her brick-wall response was always the same. It was somehow my fault that the guitar was broken, and the answer to compensation was always no. As you sometimes read about hostages and their kidnappers, I oddly enough found myself developing a bit of a crush on Ms. Irlweg through our daily encounters, until my wife warned me to smarten up and regain my perspective.

United's stance was this: something must have been wrong with my case, I had signed a damage waiver, and I waited too long to open my claim. My rebuttal was: my Taylor had traveled with two cases surrounding it for protection (a hard-shelled case and a soft nylon case to protect the skin of the hard-shell); I hadn't signed a waiver; and I reported the damage at my earliest opportunity, before being told to bring it back to Canada for inspection.

Ms. Irlweg and I danced along for maybe ten e-mail exchanges before she ended our relationship with "The Final No!" It was in one of these later-stage e-mails that I made my offer for compensation. The repair to my damaged Taylor cost me $1,200, so I suggested that I would accept $1,200 in United Airlines flight vouchers as compensation. With the vouchers, I could defray future touring expenses. For the airline, it would amount to a free settlement and an opportunity to give me a better in-flight experience and establish my loyalty to their brand. It seemed like a sound resolution to me.

Although she never disputed the events leading to my damaged Taylor, Ms. Irlweg said the fact that I did not open a claim within 24 hours was my ultimate undoing, that the answer would remain no, and that the matter was closed. What's worse, she said she would not be answering any more of my e-mails. We had officially broken up!

I was devastated! How could she do that to me? To us! I felt like I had been punched in the stomach, and I reacted by watching my fingers type out an e-mail response that would declare my intentions in the coming months. I encouraged Ms. Irlweg to reconsider because I wasn't without options. If I were a lawyer, I might sue United, but as a songwriter, I had other tools at my disposal.

As I had done in the past with previous failed relationships, I promised her that I would respond by writing a song about my experience, only I was so upset with this breakup that it would take two or three songs. I would then make a music video for each and post them on YouTube, with the intended goal of achieving a combined one million views in the next year.

I told her that she was not obligated to respond to my e-mail and that I would keep her up-to-date on my progress. When the first video was up and ready, I would invite her to watch it so that "together we might reach one million views that much sooner," and I closed by stating that my new focus would be in answering the question "Now, what rhymes with Irlweg?"

So that was it. The idea was born. After months of feeling frustrated and angry about the ordeal, for the first time I felt empowered, as though a weight had been lifted from me. I changed gears from someone who *wanted* something to someone who was going to *do* something. Contrary to popular opinion, my motivation was never to force United to compensate me. From this point on, I actually accepted that there would be no compensation and let it go.

When I chose to stop wasting time and energy navigating a customer-service maze and start investing that energy in a challenging creative project, I instantly felt better. Just the decision to take action vented months of frustration.

When I hit SEND that final time, I questioned the sanity of what I had just taken on. Nevertheless, I had declared to the universe and Ms. Irlweg what I was going to do, and I fully committed myself to doing it. I would produce three stylistically different songs and videos about my experience with United Airlines. Now, how to approach it? That was my next challenge, and the answer was rooted in the life lessons I had learned growing up.

♬ ♪ ♬ ♪ ♬

Chapter 4

DOING THE BEST WITH WHAT YOU'VE GOT

For the majority of my career, I've performed with my brother, Don, in our duo, Sons of Maxwell, and have been asked many times how we settled on that name. I'd like to be able to describe some interesting life event that led us to adopt the name Sons of Maxwell, but in reality, it's as simple as it sounds. Don and I are the sons of Max Carroll.

Our career began without any thought to a name, mostly because we weren't aware we were starting a career. I had bought a guitar while attending Carleton University in Ottawa and learned a few chords. Don and I entered a talent contest, tied for first place, and were paid $75 to come back and play a full show at the college-residence pub. Considering that being paid anything made us professional in our books, we figured we'd better choose a name for our act—so, because the band consisted of Don and me, and because we were putting on a show, we went with "the Don and Dave Show."

We soon discovered that other places would pay us to sing, and our first off-campus gig meant taking a slight pay cut to only $50, but a job well done meant that we got a $5 tip and one free beer each. As spine-tingling a name as the Don and Dave Show was, we felt we could do better in that department, but it wasn't until really committing to music as a full-time career and deciding to move to Halifax, Nova Scotia, that a new name became a priority.

Up to this point, we had been enjoying a strong following in Ottawa, but felt the Canadian East Coast music scene separated the men from the boys, especially for the pub-style Celtic music that was central to our show at the time. If we could establish ourselves in Halifax, we could enjoy a career anywhere. To help ourselves do that, we agreed we needed a new name.

In those days, we drove to gigs in our tiny pickup truck and entertained ourselves running through the endless possibilities of handles for our duo. Our objective was a name that sounded bigger than just two guys, one that identified us as brothers while reflecting a hint of the Celtic side of things. We agreed to avoid the obvious Carroll Family Singers, and kept brainstorming until Don came up with the name Sons of Maxwell, and it struck a chord.

THE BAND NAME SONS OF MAXWELL met all Don's and my criteria and simultaneously honored one of the people most responsible for our successfully earning a living playing music: our father. Music was always a big part of our lives, and some of my earliest memories include Dad visiting our room with guitar in hand to say good night to us.

Where some parents might sing a lullaby or two to put their children to sleep, my father would show up expecting a sing-along and come prepared to play a full mini-show! His sets were varied, ranging from such hits as the all-ages family favorite "There's a Hole in the Bucket," to the more mature "Tom Dooley," a song about premeditated murder . . . okay, so maybe that one wasn't such a good idea, but at least Dad's sets had variety.

When he didn't know the lyrics, he'd encourage us to make up our own. Buddy Holly was a mainstay, but it wasn't until much later that I realized that we'd never actually sung all of "Peggy Sue" or that he hadn't known the right chords to many of the songs.

Our dad never worried about having all the lyrics committed to memory or lifting the arrangement note for note from a record. Even today, a crime-scene investigator would be hard-pressed to find a single fingerprint of Dad's on the black keys of our piano. Ironically, every song he knows is in the key of C and has three or four chords, so he's never needed those extra keys. For bedtime concerts, he'd play a cheap guitar and sing only the best parts of each song he liked, before moving on to the next one.

You see, he was interested in experiencing the music with his sons, not waiting until it was perfected before playing his music for others. In fact, his philosophy was quite simple: "If you don't know the music, sing louder, and if you don't know the words, play louder!" Long before Nike ever said "Just do it," Dad was living that philosophy. The result is that I have great memories of going to bed wound up tight—and getting less sleep than I probably should have—but nevertheless fully entertained.

In most of the successful things I've done in my life, that same philosophy has been a cornerstone in getting started. Several times I recall Don and me, as an opening act with our one guitar and two voices, receiving a more enthusiastic response from large crowds than the headlining bands that followed us.

We didn't wait until we had the best instruments, or even wait until I knew how to play my instrument well. We just did it and involved our audience in a shared experience that allowed us to work as professional musicians as we learned our craft, on the job. While some bands "show" audiences what they do, we learned early on to *share* what we do. Achieving our goal of connecting with others is what made us successful, while other bands, with better musicianship, struggled because their objective was to show audiences how good they were.

We learned a lot during that formative "zygote period" playing cover songs in the Ottawa pub circuit, but those early successes were founded upon the lessons learned much earlier at the bedtime sing-alongs. I continue to draw from them today in both my songwriting and solo career, and when I committed to the United Airlines trilogy, those lessons would be central in my approach and largely responsible for the videos' success.

So to recap, before July 6, 2009, before creating "United Breaks Guitars" ("UBG"), I was strictly an independent singer-songwriter. I had just released my solo CD, but my career until then had revolved around singing for my supper and writing and recording songs for Sons of Maxwell shows.

Within the music industry, success for a musician is defined by awards, box-office receipts, music sales, or having someone really famous recording your music (so that you earn a royalty on the strength of that individual's career). I had experienced highs and lows in most of those areas, but I personally believe that success is defined by your ability to earn a living doing what you love. Until 2009, I had done that with one band for 20 years, and for that reason, I was successful . . . by my own definition, at least.

There'll never be a shortage of music-industry experts with the formula for success, and while some my brother and I have encountered continue to do great things, others are now bankrupt. Don and I, for better or worse, did what we had to do to remain employed in the music business. Where some would insist that the road to the next level demands focusing on only one genre and being one thing to avoid confusion ("You need to be either a pub band or an original band"), we developed into a versatile group with the ability to play an all-original theater show one night and a thousand-person beer tent the next.

We believed that doing a good job on any stage, as often as possible, was the way up. Some of our audience members occasionally left confused, but only in the form of the question "I don't know why you guys aren't famous yet." Our approach was successful in that it allowed us to stave off the dreaded day job (tantamount to cancer for music careers everywhere).

Once "UBG" hit it big on YouTube, some of the media reports portrayed me as more of a wannabe musician than an actual professional in the industry.

Maybe that portrayal added to the warmth of the story, but the truth is that Don and I enjoyed plenty of success and travel as an independent band. We've won awards and received critical acclaim, and have been some people's favorite band in the world for quite a while. As a result of being around so long, and touring the world with our music, we would sometimes run into fans in the unlikeliest of places. We've toured the U.S., Canada, and the Caribbean; made several trips to Germany; and even played as far away as China.

On that China trip, we were part of a six-band delegation from Canada, and we performed in several cities. With us were Jordan Cook, the Rheostatics, Forever, Stradio, and a saxophone trio called the Shuffle Demons (who brought a camera crew with them to cover their trip). The Chinese, known to make sweeping statements, advertised our collective as "The Six Most Popular Bands in North America!" I was impressed and shocked that it took coming to China to find this out, but we did our best to rise to the occasion.

At the end of the tour, we were able to go to the Great Wall near Beijing for a visit. It was incredible, and you're allowed to walk a section of the Wall only as far as a designated guard tower atop a flat section on the mountain. It's a bit of a climb to get there, and by the time we arrived at that final lookout atop the guard tower, the Shuffle Demons had set up their camera to say hello to their fans back in Canada.

It felt like they were broadcasting from the moon, with us being so far away from home. I recall that just as they had begun filming that scene, they were interrupted by someone from around the corner who yelled out, "Hey! Sons of Maxwell!" It turned out that a fan of our band from Fredericton, New Brunswick, Canada, was in China at the same time taking a tour of the Great Wall. Social media was still a couple of years from really catching on, so we laughed as we realized the Shuffle

Demons broadcast from so far away was a lot closer to home than we realized.

It seemed like we had come a long way from some early gigs that were not nearly as magical and mystical as that meeting on the Great Wall of China. One that springs to mind, of early times and earlier struggles, happened at the beginning of our career when we had only played maybe six shows and returned home from college to get summer jobs.

We were hired to play a community parking-lot party on Canada Day in a smaller town near our hometown of Timmins, Ontario. The event was billed as "fun for the whole family," but that wasn't exactly how it turned out. The local bar obtained an expanded liquor license and set up a fenced-in beer garden to the side of the flatbed trailer Don and I would use as a stage. Everyone in town was invited, but the problem was that the bar was sketchy, with an even sketchier clientele. So by showtime that night, only the bar's regulars were there, and they stayed inside the beer garden.

We played facing a completely empty parking lot and were verbally abused for two hours by people from the beer garden who didn't appreciate our one-guitar-two-voices-pop-folk show. Ozzy Osbourne might have been too tame for that crowd. Instead of ignoring them for just a little longer and finishing the gig, I decided to say something unkind over the microphone to one specific offender. He was particularly put out by my comment, and it all went downhill from there.

It was soon apparent we needed to leave that town right away, and coincidentally, the town suffered a blackout at exactly the same time. As we tried to collect our instruments, and money, in the dark before beer bottles started raining down on us, Don's girlfriend pulled up in the getaway car and parked in front of the stage. As she sat there revving the engine and blinding the beer-garden people with the car's high beams, they appeared confused as we loaded the Volvo and accepted a police escort out of town. I've never been back to that particular northern Ontario town, and I'm glad we put that one behind us early.

So we took the ups and downs, the highs and lows; and like most people, I found that after 20 years my outlook on life changed a bit. In 2008, my wife, Jill, became pregnant with our son, Flynn. As a first-time parent, I now had someone else depending on me to be around, and I began to question the value in being away from home. Essentially I had been living week to week for my entire career, and even though I had a good streak going of making ends meet for over a thousand straight weeks, supplementing what I felt were more meaningful gigs by playing bars was not as enjoyable for me anymore. I began to question how much time away from home I could justify, singing my own songs or someone else's. If I wasn't as busy as I needed to be doing the kind of shows I was most passionate about, then maybe it was time to do something else.

As it turned out, in 2005 Don and I had become proud members of the Station 41 Volunteer Fire Department where we lived in Waverley, Nova Scotia, just outside Halifax. We enjoyed the experience of going to emergency calls to help others, so in 2008, when Halifax announced that they were recruiting full-time firefighters, we decided to apply along with 900 other people. We passed all the testing, and I made it through my first-ever job interview.

Later that year, Don was selected ahead of me in the first group of 20 candidates, embracing this "day job" concept that we had only heard people talk about. I was placed on a list for hiring in the near future. Sons of Maxwell was no longer a full-time, anytime band, so I would rely on the group and my solo career until I too would transition to a job with benefits and a pension.

My first passion would always be music, but if making a change was the best thing for my family, then I was grateful that my fallback plan was one of the most respected professions in the world and something I also loved doing. And that was my plan . . . until life dealt me some different cards, and my whole world turned upside down.

♬ ♪ ♬ ♪ ♬

Part II

THE MAKING OF THE "UBG" TRILOGY

Chapter 5

"UNITED BREAKS GUITARS" IS CREATED

So with my commitment made to the universe and Ms. Irlweg, I knew that before I could write and record a trilogy of songs, I had to write the first one. It was in January 2009 that I sat down to pen what would become "United Breaks Guitars" ("UBG"). Sometimes when I sit down to write a song, I find it useful to think about what I'm trying to accomplish as a whole. What is the purpose of this song, and what am I attempting to convey? Knowing where I want to end up when I'm done demands that I know where to start so I can make the right adjustments along the way.

I decided to consider my purpose for the entire trilogy before I started writing that first song, and this made a world of difference in the final product. I had accepted that I would not receive any compensation from United for the damage, so why was I doing this? It was clear to me that my purpose for the "UBG" trilogy would be threefold:

First, I would take a frustrating experience and turn it into a positive one with my music. I'm passionate about songwriting and love the process. By committing to not just one song but three of them, each being a different perspective on the same story, I was challenging myself artistically. Even if no one else ever heard these songs, I would become a better songwriter for it, so my measure of success was always within reach.

Second, I wanted to bring my friends together to manifest these songs into real living, breathing music videos. I enjoy this process immensely and considered that this project might be something that my friends and I could reflect upon someday as a great way to have spent some time.

Third, I considered what might happen if the videos became successful. Although I could never have imagined how successful "UBG" would become, I felt that if enough people watched the videos, they could potentially compel one of the world's largest companies to change the way it deals with customers. If that happened, was it possible that others might follow suit?

This third consideration was beyond my control, so I listed it as a "long-shot outcome" and focused on what I *could* control. I would involve my friends in making something that looked good, sounded good, and made people want to tell their friends about it.

Knowing that the Internet is a noisy environment where attention spans are short and competition for that attention is fierce, I needed a song that would engage people immediately and hold their interest. I compare the atmosphere on the Internet to the bustling pubs where Don and I used to perform. When a pub was packed with people drinking and talking, and we hoped to cut through the noise, we discovered that certain kinds of songs work better than others. If you want to engage the audience quickly, then something fast and familiar does the trick every time!

People have difficulty ignoring a strong, steady beat and a song that they can sing along with. So as a song-writer who tends to write the music before the lyrics, I decided that the template for "UBG" would be an up-tempo train groove (with a "boom-chug-a-lugga-lugga" feel). A lot of Johnny Cash songs, like "Ring of Fire" and "Folsom Prison Blues," have that going on, and it really works. I had the groove figured out.

In many of the interviews I've done since the release of "UBG," I've been introduced as "country singer Dave Carroll." The truth is, although I love country music and have always had more subtle elements of it in my writing, I am nowhere near as country as "UBG" would suggest. Making "UBG" so country was a choice and done for good reason.

Classic country songs tend to be about hurt and loss, and with my United experience, where to take my song musically was a no-brainer. I would try to make "United Breaks Guitars" a faithful homage to the likes of Marty Robbins and Hank Williams in the style of a good old-fashioned hurtin' song. I had settled on my theme.

Another element of a great tune that cuts through the noise is a strong chorus. The chorus of a well-written song is the part that is unforgettable after one listen and contains the most energy, as well as the essence of the message. That's a tall order for a few seconds of music and one reason why good songwriting is an art.

The chorus has to be energetic, clear, and memorable. I've enjoyed the experience many times leading a packed venue in song, where most people may only know the lyrics to the chorus. They do their best to muddle through the verses with you, so excited to get to that part they know that their lips mouth words that don't even exist in English. When the chorus hits, they erupt into something more akin to a yell-along than a sing-along, and it's an awesome experience to be holding the reins on that when it happens. I wanted to tailor a song that might have that same effect.

STRUCTURALLY, I DECIDED MY SONG would be a narrative. I would tell the facts of the story truthfully, since there was no need to embellish. The truth held enough drama and tension that I didn't have to make anything up, so I decided the verses would lay out the facts as though I were reporting a crime to the police.

I would have the lyrics in the verses skip along, telling the story at a lively pace until they ran head-on into the part I wanted people never to forget: the chorus. At that point the energy rises, the tempo stays the same, but the lyrical pace slows, so that the listener has no question about what I'm saying: "United! United! You broke my Taylor guitar!" (You can explore the full lyrics to all three UBG songs, which I have included at the end of the book.)

The rich three-part harmony background vocals you hear in the video were always in the front of my mind when writing the song. I knew they would add excitement to the chorus and give some authenticity to the style they used back in the 1950s on those old Marty Robbins tunes. I recall laughing out loud, working out those harmony parts as I envisioned the classic background singers of the day voicing those long, drawn-out phrases, while seemingly scanning a distant sunset. That definitely had to be part of the song!

Once I was clear on the framework, the song pretty much wrote itself, and it was completed in two days. My wife, Jill, awoke that first morning and discovered me in the living room playing guitar and chuckling to myself. She said, "What are you laughing about?"

"I'm working on my United song," I replied with a giggle, the first of many similar high-energy moments with this project. It was a far cry from my frame of mind when I was stuck inside the United customer-service maze.

RECORDING SONGS TODAY is a much different process than it used to be. Everything used to be recorded in big chunks at one very expensive studio, but today home studios are affordable for most, and the various musical parts can be recorded remotely and assembled (mixed) later. That was how "UBG" came to be. I recorded my acoustic guitar and all the singing parts in my basement office. Bass player Jamie Gatti also recorded there. I then called on my friend and producer of my *Perfect Blue* recording, Jamie Robinson, to lay down some electric guitar.

After explaining the approach I was after, Jamie delivered a great track on his Telecaster electric to give it a truly authentic sound. He recorded his parts at his house and e-mailed me the tracks when they were done. I then called my friend Scott Ferguson, who not only drums with our band whenever possible, but also owns his own studio called Ferguson Music Productions.

Scott agreed to donate his services and his studio to lay down the groove and mix all the parts together. This entire project rested on the strength of the song, and without everyone's help the production would not have been as rich and musically strong. Thanks to the players, the foundation of the whole project was rock solid (or in this case "country solid").

When I had the song mixed and mastered, I sent it to my film-industry friends at Curve Productions in Halifax (Lara Cassidy, Steve Richard, and Chris Pauley). I explained that United had broken my guitar and refused to take responsibility for it, so my response would be to make three music videos; would they help me? Without hesitation they said, "Okay, what's your budget?"

I replied, "Zero dollars. Is that a problem?"

After a slight hesitation, they said, "Okay, we can give you a one-day shoot, and we'll have a small crew. We'll do the best we can and see what happens." The Curve Productions video crew ended up consisting of Lara, Steve, and Chris—along with Joshua Young and Barb Richard—and they did a phenomenal job with limited resources.

With no budget for lighting, we needed a free outside location, so as a volunteer firefighter in Waverley, I asked my chief if I could use the fire-hall parking lot for our outside shots. He said okay, so we picked a day in late May 2009 and hoped for good weather.

The next move was to find cast members, a job that was split between Curve Productions and me. I called my brother, Don, and reminded him about that song I'd written about United, and asked if he wanted to be in the video. Unfortunately, he had to decline. Many people have asked why my brother wasn't in the video, and some have suspected a deeper, acrimonious reason, but it was that simple: as a full-time firefighter, he had to work! Never thinking things would take off as they did, he wished me luck, and I put the call out to three musician friends.

I phoned Mike Hiltz (bass player), Chris Iannetti (electric guitarist), and Jimmie Inch (songwriter) and quickly explained: "United broke my guitar, and I'm writing three songs about it. We're shooting the first video next week. I can't pay you anything, but do you want to be a background singer and dress up like a mariachi guy, and wear a fake mustache and sombrero?"

Without hesitation they all said, "Okay." I love how musicians don't need all the details before saying yes to a gig.

None of them had done any acting, but I had a hunch that my Three Amigos would be perfect, and they were! Each of them brought a hilarious expression or gesture to the video that cracked us up more than once. Nothing says funny like a blond-haired guy with a phony thick black mustache. In fact, you can see us attempting to contain our laughter at several points throughout the final YouTube version.

We needed baggage handlers next, and I looked to the volunteer fire department for them. I asked two guys from my station, Charlie Palmer and Phil Salterio, and they too jumped on board without hesitation. I love how volunteer firefighters don't need all the details before saying yes to a gig. Phil and Charlie are both bigger guys and looked perfect for the part. We dressed them up in our firefighting coveralls and used the fire-department hearing-protection headphones and rubber mallets as props. They did a great job.

One of my favorite scenes is the profile shot of Charlie, lined up to catch the guitar like a baseball catcher awaiting a throw to home, only the guitar goes whizzing past him, with the throw nowhere close. There were funny behind-the-scenes moments as well. I recall Phil, forgetting he was there to "act," spinning around with the guitar case to simulate a throw and actually sending the case 30 feet in Olympic hammer toss–style, almost destroying our prop and damaging a few cars! As Charlie said, "You have to talk nice and slow to the big guy."

In my role as casting director, my next big find was Christine Buiteman. She too had no acting experience, but as a longtime friend, I called her at work in the Nova Scotia music-industry office and said, "Hey, Christine, United broke my guitar, and we're shooting a music video about it next week. I can't pay you, but I need you to play two roles: a flight attendant and the customer-service rep who denied my claim."

She said "Okay." I love how music-industry professionals don't need all the details before saying yes to a gig.

Steve Richard is an accomplished commercial photographer, in addition to his job with Curve Productions, so I asked him if he could find two models he had maybe worked with before who could play the other flight attendants. He called Karen Murdoch and Paula Robbins, and they agreed to be part of our project. Like me, Steve loves models who don't need to know all the details of a gig before saying yes . . . and we finally had our full cast! I was blown away by everyone's contributions, and the enthusiasm was infectious, making the day unbelievably fun.

THE WEATHER ENDED UP COOPERATING and providing us with a beautiful spring day, so we were able to complete all the outdoor shots by lunchtime. We made good use of the few props we had. I collected as many empty suitcases as possible, and we placed them around the parking lot for effect. The guitar used in the video is not the one that was damaged on my flight. In fact, it's not even a Taylor. By then my guitar had been repaired, and the actual damage would have been difficult to see on camera anyway. I called a local music retailer and asked my friend in the repair department if he had any guitars beyond hope that I could destroy for a music video. He gave me one that had been collecting dust in the back room, so I brought it home and smashed the headstock off with a rubber mallet. It surprised me how many times I had to hit it to break the neck.

I also bought some sidewalk chalk that ended up being used in a defining moment in the video. I suggested we place the broken guitar on the ground like a victim at a murder scene and draw a chalk outline around it to simulate a dead body. Countless people e-mailed to say they loved that bit, and I have since made that chalk outline the logo for my company Big Break Enterprises Inc. The chalk outline also reprises its role at the end of "United Breaks Guitars: Song Two" ("UBG2").

Throughout the day, we had a few general ideas as to what we wanted to see, but much of it was done on the fly, with maybe one rehearsal and one or two takes before moving on to the next shot. As a result, everything came across very authentic and unrehearsed, adding to the organic feel of the video.

After completing the outdoor shots, we headed into Halifax to Steve Richard's photo studio to do all the indoor filming. Steve had this idea of shooting a scene from the outside of a homemade fuselage and capturing the passengers' expressions from the window. I had my reservations about how that would look, but when I got to the studio, I was sold! Steve's wife, Barb, is a talented artist whose specialties include painting and creating stained-glass pieces, so she was obviously overqualified for this project when Steve enlisted her to build us a white foam-core fuselage with three windows.

It looks convincing on-screen, but in reality it was hilarious. Clamps suspended a 4 × 8 sheet of foam-core with holes cut out for windows and rivets drawn in with marker. When we sat in the chairs behind it to look out the windows, from the front you could see our legs and feet along the bottom, as though the plane were some mode of transportation on *The Flintstones*.

The studio scenes were shot in roughly four hours but included important pieces in the storytelling. I wanted to make use of the old *Road Runner* cartoon tactic of using handheld signs on sticks to communicate a message, so we had fun making those and using them to full advantage. I spent hours creating the 18-inch airplane cutout that makes a four-second appearance in the video. It was my first movie prop, after all, and needed to look great. So in four hours at Steve's studio, we filmed the campy fuselage scene.

Another favorite for me was the funeral scene where the Three Amigos and I change wardrobes into black funeral suits, with the guitar resting peacefully in its velvet-lined case/casket. We introduced Ms. Irlweg (complete with name tag) as United's bearer of bad news. We captured the looks of indifference by the three employees in Chicago and had fun with the standard performance footage of me singing the story. It all went by quickly, and I remember leaving the studio at 6 P.M.

feeling that regardless of who might see the video, we had done something pretty special that day.

As it turned out, with the help of a few friends and $150, we produced a song and a music video that has been enjoyed by millions and changed the world in measurable ways. No one had acting experience. We were sorely lacking in proper equipment and had only a skeleton film crew. We were rushed for time and had next to no rehearsals. We had no distribution for the video aside from a hope that, when it was done, maybe someone on YouTube would want to watch it and tell a friend.

As has happened so many times in my career, there were plenty of reasons to wait until all the conditions were better in order to move ahead. But once again, I took a leap of faith that doing the best you can with what you've got always leaves you better off than having done nothing at all. I was reminded that stepping up to make the most of an opportunity is when magic occurs and that the right people will always appear for you, at just the right time, but you have to first show up yourself.

It was the same lesson I had learned from my dad's bedtime sing-alongs so many years before: that music connects us and sharing your experience is not only more enjoyable for others, but it also changes your own experience for the better. Personally, I enjoyed the experience of making the video infinitely more by watching my friends enjoy the process, and their contributions made the video better than I ever could have managed on my own. Funny how that works, isn't it? And how unfortunate that we don't do this more often!

Before I leave this chapter, I have to send a shout-out to Lara Cassidy, who deserves the accolades for taking on the role of video editor as well as director. Because we had so few takes for her to consider in the edit suite, I think she did a superb job of meticulously going over each second of footage to find the best part to tell the story. Her greatest challenge was probably trying to find a scene that worked but didn't include someone bursting out laughing, and there are quite a few clips where she had to strategically cut to another clip just before we busted up—again.

Lara did a brilliant job with the editing process, and she was one of the people on my team who did see the bigger picture. Within weeks of the release of "UBG," Lara approached a major Canadian TV broadcaster about funding a documentary about the experience. We had been keeping some behind-the-scenes video, and we also had footage of later trips to California and Washington where I spoke about my experiences. Lara had access to the whole story, and the documentary would have been excellent.

However, the broadcasting executive who listened to Lara explain the history and what was going on as a result of the video and the potential impacts ahead calmly dismissed the idea as being nothing more than another YouTube video, not unlike a cat that can flush a toilet.

One more time we saw how some of the traditional media outlets are blind to what's going on right under their noses. My ego was a little bruised by the association to toilet-flushing felines, but I quickly got over it when I realized how cutting-edge "UBG" really was. This woman was probably good at what she knew, but there were no experts (yet!) in the emerging field of "independent YouTube music videos relaying a message with a global impact."

As I have come to learn, some people can only understand what they've seen before, so I know I shouldn't hold it against that executive for not being able to see the bigger picture that was still being created. As it turned out, another Toronto company called Generator Films has since done a documentary on customer service with a different broadcaster that features "UBG" heavily. Sometimes that's just how the cookie crumbles.

But fortunately, I was able to surround myself with a team of friends who shared my enthusiasm and vision to do something unique. Within hours of posting "UBG" to YouTube, "we few, we happy few" would embark on the ride of a lifetime.

♫ ♪ ♫ ♪ ♫

Chapter 6

LIFE IN A MEDIA FRENZY

When our director, Lara Cassidy, sent me the final edit of the "United Breaks Guitars" video, it was Canada Day, July 1, 2009, which is a national public holiday like the American Independence Day. I was instructing at a songwriting camp not far from Halifax at the time, and I was thrilled to get the video. I thought it had turned out great, but after seeing so many edited versions and being so involved, I wondered if I might be biased.

Was it really that funny? Would anyone want to share it with a friend? I decided to test-market the video that night, so I brought my laptop to the camp bunkhouse and showed the video to some of the other songwriters there to gauge their reaction and get feedback. I couldn't have been more pleased. They laughed at all the right places and more. When the video was done, they wanted to watch it again and called others into the room to share the experience.

After everyone had seen it, I noticed that conversations were starting about everyone's own bad airline experiences. It was my first inkling that I might have touched on something big. As a songwriter, however, I'm always concerned with the reaction to any of my work when I first present it, so I was more relieved that my fellow songwriters didn't hate the song.

What I didn't know was that Lara hadn't just sent me a private version of the video; she actually posted it to Facebook as well. I hadn't spent any time considering a strategy of how we'd share the video when it was ready, but I asked her to take it down until we could formulate a more detailed plan when I got home.

When the camp had concluded and I had returned home, it was Monday night, July 6. I hadn't come up with anything better than Lara's strategy of simply posting it for others to see, so that night I decided to use the Max Carroll and Nike approach of "Just do it." I asked my website administrator, Ryan Moore, if he wouldn't mind posting the video to our existing Sons of Maxwell YouTube channel, and he had it posted shortly after, at 11:30 P.M. When I confirmed that it worked and was up and running, I sent a message to 600 friends on Facebook and an e-mail to everyone on my Outlook Express contact list.

My goal was to reach one million hits with all three videos combined in the next year. Thirty minutes into my campaign, I had a total of six. I was under the impression that every one of those six hits were my own, and I figured that if I had to watch this thing 999,994 more times, I'd probably need some rest, so I went to sleep at midnight. That was my entire social-media master plan: send two messages and go to bed! It's worth noting that July 6 was the only time I've actively asked people to watch that first video, which today sits at 11.4 million hits. Since then, it's been driven completely by word of mouth, along with social and mainstream media.

I discovered sometime later that in reality, one YouTube hit constitutes the acknowledgment that a single IP address has viewed a video, and it is never counted a second time. So if you were to watch "UBG" multiple times from your home, it would only ever count as one hit. With so many messages from people claiming that watching the video is a daily ritual, the implication is that the number of views far exceeds the number of hits and that when I went to bed on July 6 with six hits, five other IP addresses had already contributed to the count. The power of social media had shown itself, and I wasn't even aware of it at the time.

WHEN I AWOKE ON TUESDAY MORNING, the YouTube counter read 300 hits. I was thrilled at the thought that someone else had watched and that maybe I could do other things besides hit PLAY on my laptop repeatedly for the next 364 days . . . and since I enjoy other things, like eating and breathing, this was good.

I immediately called my friend Steve Richard, the director of photography for the video, and true to his conservative disposition, he said, "Don't get too excited. This could be over by noon."

But it wasn't over by noon. By noon, the video had reached 5,000 hits. By dinnertime, it reached 25,000 and was gaining traction on notable pro-consumer websites such as *The Consumerist.* That morning, I did my first interview about the video with the Halifax *Chronicle Herald* newspaper and was told it would appear online that day and in Wednesday's paper. Following the interview, I left for a performance with Sons of Maxwell we'd scheduled for that night in Stellarton, Nova Scotia, which was roughly a two-hour drive from Halifax, so I couldn't follow the video's progress until after the show.

That night the band played "UBG" at the gig, and I told the background story of how it came to be, explaining to the conference audience of 500 fire chiefs and their spouses that the video was available to be viewed on YouTube. I noticed that the reaction from this demographic was identical to the completely different audience I'd first shown it to at the songwriter camp. It was encouraging in that the song seemed to resonate with all ages.

When the gig was over and I left the stage, there was a message waiting on my cell phone from the *Los Angeles Times*. They had picked up the online story posted by the *Herald* earlier that day and wanted some more details. I gave the reporter an interview and was told that it would be posted in the online overnight version of the paper and in the physical edition on Wednesday. I recall driving home that night and considering the possibilities of how this video might really take off and wondered if any other credible media would be interested in interviews in the coming weeks.

Everything changed that next day, starting at 6 A.M. when Jill and I were awakened by a phone call from a local radio station, C100, to talk about my video. Excited by the news that it had started to go viral, I finished the interview, and we got out of bed to check the YouTube count, discovering that it had continued to rise exponentially overnight.

Not only that, my e-mail in-box was overflowing with congratulations from supporters and inquiries for interviews. The phone began ringing off the hook, and it wasn't just my home line, but both my cell and Jill's as well. The interview requests were pouring in, and we simply couldn't keep up.

I was giving phone interviews to media from around the world and then answering questions online. There were so many Facebook comments and incoming messages that we could only consider replying to those that asked a direct question and had to ignore the deluge of encouraging statements. We set up my e-mail account with an auto-reply that apologized for any delay in responding, which remained in place for months as we attempted to revisit unanswered messages and keep up with the incoming ones.

Jill and I had just become first-time parents three months earlier, and we were still exhausted from that alone. When the video hit, we were really struggling to keep up, and I recall realizing we were officially overwhelmed on day three when I was giving an interview and I looked across the kitchen to Jill, who was setting up an interview with someone on her phone, replying to an e-mail, and breast-feeding Flynn at the same time. There's nothing I respect more than the ability to multitask, so right there, I fell in love all over again . . . but I also surrendered to the fact that we needed help.

A small core team developed around me very quickly. My friend and part-time drummer Julian Marentette phoned the house when it was apparent this was catching fire and offered any assistance we might need. At the time, he was working for the Canadian Cancer Society, and when I filled him in on the scope of what was happening, he offered to take a leave of absence from his job to become my right-hand man and help manage things.

I gratefully accepted, and for the next month Julian was a terrific help, and he and I saw a lot of each other.

Jill's father, Brent Sansom, was our next call. Brent had been an executive in the telecom sector for his entire career and was in semiretirement at that time, so Jill phoned in an SOS. My father-in-law arrived from his home in Moncton, New Brunswick, the next day and lived with us for two months. For nearly two years, he has continued to devote his energy to my cause as we tried to understand and embrace the many implications and opportunities "UBG" had created.

Like most independent musicians, I ran a business that was home based and a 100 percent do-it-yourself operation. I had no manager, agent, publicist, administrative assistant, or music distribution, but with the efficient use of my time, I was doing well to run things until then. I wasn't prepared for what was unfolding now, though, so I made the snap executive decision to double the size of my operation. Brent drove to Walmart and bought a couple of card tables and a two-line phone. I also broke the bank and invested in a whiteboard and an assortment of colored markers.

At this time, I didn't have a Twitter account, let alone know what a "tweet" was. Johanna Harrison, who has since become my social-media advisor, among other things, walked Jill through the sign-up process from her home base in Timmins, Ontario. Twitter traffic began to take off before I really understood what Twitter was and why I should have it. I was told, "Don't question it, just tweet" . . . so I did, and added that to the growing list of on-the-job learning experiences.

With my team assembled, my kitchen had been turned into a command center. The whiteboard was getting a workout, keeping track of media requests according to category: Hard News, Travel, Human Interest, Business, Entertainment, and Social Media. There was barely enough room in the house to move with all the activity, and I recall being impressed that everyone seemed to have something to do and was doing it. My job was to keep telling the story, so I felt a bit like a fly on the wall of my own adventure.

One of the turning points in that first week came on Wednesday when CNN called and then e-mailed with an interview request. I gave the interview to a reporter, who thanked me for my time and said the segment might air that night if they decided to run it at all. The rest of the day was filled with calls and e-mails, so I didn't think much about it, since that evening I was appearing on the number one regional news show in Atlantic Canada, called *Live at 5*.

I was thinking about the large market share this show commands at nearly 500,000 viewers, and as we were coming out of a commercial break to start the interview, Starr Dobson, the *Live at 5* co-host, ran up to say, "You're on *The Situation Room with Wolf Blitzer* right now!" That was surreal.

When I got home, the atmosphere was electric. My family and friends were there, and my home felt more like the campaign headquarters on a victorious election night. The phone was ringing, and family and friends kept arriving at the house to share in the experience. There was laughing and hugging; people were eating finger sandwiches and casseroles (the food of celebrations and funerals). There was a real sense that something big was afoot.

Jill had taped as many of the day's TV interviews as she could find, and we sat together and watched the significant CNN piece with Wolf Blitzer as he smiled and rocked out to the video (for Wolf that entails some extremely subtle shoulder pumping, but I saw it; it required slo-mo, but it was there). The "United Breaks Guitars" story, with extreme close-ups of my friends in their sombreros and mustaches, was on the big *Situation Room* screens, and the feature about us was bookended by stories on the Pope and Barack Obama. Things really took off from there. "UBG" had gone from a music video to a "Situation" . . . CNN had just said so, and they are the self-proclaimed most trusted name in news.

Most of my interviews that first week were phoners or done online, but I also did several television spots for regional stations in what they call double-enders. A double-ender is a remote interview that is done in one studio and beamed by satellite to another. The CTV station in Halifax has a room in the back of the studio that is used for just such things and can be essentially hired out by other networks to acquire these interviews, so CTV was a regular stop for double-enders in the first few weeks of "UBG."

Good Morning America was one of my first double-enders. I had to learn quickly how to handle these types of interviews. Every room that I've been in for a double-ender looks similar. They are small spaces containing a chair, a mural for a backdrop, a camera, a camera operator, and an earpiece. You might imagine that there would be a TV monitor so that you could see the person you're talking to, but because there is a transmission delay, such a monitor would be distracting.

The approach for me was to simply listen to the question through my earpiece and look directly into the camera as though it were the other person. That feels unnatural, and it's not easy to do; but it's important, because if your eyes wander, it's very distracting to the viewer, and you can appear shifty. As a general rule, I prefer to avoid looking shifty whenever possible, so I worked hard to always look at the camera when considering my answers to these on-the-spot questions.

In the first two weeks of the video's release, Julian and I were inseparable, aside from sleeping (Jill insisted that he had to go home at night). His job was to take the interview requests, schedule them in the appointment book, and join me for all live interviews and television spots. During one of the early days, I had just finished an in-studio interview at Global Television in Halifax and was en route to do a double-ender across town at CTV minutes later. While driving to CTV, I was giving an interview to someone on my cell phone, with Julian sitting in the passenger seat of my Honda Fit taking interview requests on *his* cell phone.

Those were exciting times because you never knew who was going to call next, so when Julian's phone rang, even though my hands were full at the time, I couldn't help trying to listen to his conversation. At one point, while simultaneously driving and giving an interview, I was able to gather that Bob Taylor was on Julian's line. Fans of Taylor guitars would liken that to God calling you on the phone.

I nearly had a coronary when I heard Julian interrupt Bob to say that he would call him back, before taking another incoming call. Essentially, he hung up on

Bob Taylor! In protest, I just about drove Julian's side of the car into a telephone pole, but instead I muted my phone (since I was still doing my own interview on my cell) and then chastised him for hanging up on Bob.

Julian interjected with a whisper and a grin, "Yeah, but we have *David Letterman* on the line!"

I replied with a matching grin and a stern, "Well, okay, then," but insisted he call Bob back right away. I think the technical term for what was happening to me internally is called a "full-scale freak-out" as I listened to one side of the conversation about performing on *Letterman.*

The good news about having a viral video is that everyone wants to talk to you. The bad news is that everyone wants an exclusive. For a few days, it looked as though I'd travel to New York City to be on *Letterman, Live with Regis and Kelly,* and the *Huckabee* show on Fox, but none of those happened in the end. The *Letterman* schedule was full, and they were concerned about it being yesterday's news if they had me on a week later. Apparently I was bumped from the spot they were considering for me by Paul McCartney, which in itself is another career highlight. Fox had heard that "United Breaks Guitars: Song Two" had been written, so they insisted that Mike Huckabee's show would only be available if we performed "UBG2" (with Huckabee playing bass with me). Since the video had not even been filmed yet, we refused, and they did, too. I don't know what happened with *Live with Regis and Kelly,* but I expect that the studio felt they had been scooped, so they bailed as well.

Normally that much simultaneous rejection would change a man, but fortunately there were plenty of other cool things happening to take their place. Instead of going to New York City, Julian and I flew to California at the invitation of Taylor Guitars to tour their factory in El Cajon, near San Diego. We were also told that it had been the folks at Taylor who had asked Kevin Bacon to contact David Letterman's people on my behalf to suggest they have me on the show. I am now only two degrees of separation from Kevin Bacon, and anyone reading this is only three!

Chalise Zolezzi, the public-relations representative for Taylor Guitars, facilitated a full schedule of interviews while in San Diego, including a double-ender with the *Today* show on NBC in New York. She also brought us to L.A. for a stop at CNN Hollywood, where I did an interview in a studio next to Larry King's, and we were green-room guests during a taping of the *Jimmy Kimmel Live!* show.

Bob Taylor was away that weekend, but we were given a tour of the plant and got to see firsthand why the company is so successful. The quality of the materials, tools, and technology combines with an incredible staff of people committed to making world-class guitars. At the end of the tour, I was brought to a room containing the many models of Taylor guitars hanging on a large wall. Chalise smiled and said, "Take your time, Dave, and pick two when you're done!" Taylor had certainly enjoyed some positive attention thanks to the video, but they floored me by showing their gratitude with not one but *two* incredible gifts.

I picked an 810ce, which is very similar to my broken 710ce, and I use the 810ce as my primary stage and studio guitar now. I don't recall having the same instant affection for this new 810 as I did in the store when I bought my 710, but then again, I was being watched. It's hard to fall in love under a microscope. For my second pick, I chose an electric model. I don't really play electric guitar very often, but I was drawn to this sexy wine-colored T3 with a Bigsby tremolo arm (think B.B. King), and I thought, *If they're going to give me two, I might as well get an electric!* That was a pretty incredible moment. Not only did we make new friends at Taylor Guitars, but Chalise is now firmly entrenched on my list of favorite Americans, and I went home with two new world-class instruments.

About this same time, Ryan Moore of Rockit Development had been working hard to restart our crashing website, which could not keep up with the incredible volume of traffic. We had nowhere near the capacity to handle the influx of visitors, so Ryan was forced to keep removing elements of our site to allow for more traffic.

Even with a bare-bones website, it was still crashing, and Ryan was working round the clock to keep it up and running. All the effort we had put into developing an interactive site that offered video clips, audio clips, and photos had been reduced to some bio information and the link to the online store to buy the single of "United Breaks Guitars" and my other music.

In the week following the release of "UBG," we arranged what I call the meeting of the minds. We were given access to the boardroom at the Music Nova Scotia office, so we decided to invite respected people from different professions and industries together in an attempt to make sense of it all and where this could lead.

Julian and Brent were there, of course, with insight on big organizations and big business. We invited Tim

Hardy, the regional representative from the songwriters' royalty organization called SOCAN. Mickey Quase—a former band manager of one of Canada's most successful groups and current administrator of a provincial government department to support the music industry—was there, as was Mike Campbell. Mike owns The Carleton, Halifax's finest venue to listen to songwriters, and he was also the host of a long-running national MuchMusic television program.

Neal Alderson worked for a large East Coast PR firm and brought that expertise to the room. Christine Buiteman (aka Ms. Irlweg in our video) was there in her day-job capacity as a music-industry expert. My brother, Don, was also there, because he has a particularly acute Spidey sense, and I figured he would be able to weigh any potential new career opportunities they might suggest against the person he knew me to be.

The initial concern among the group gathered there was how to manage the media. Neal offered great advice and was active in finding ways to keep the story current and in the news. I was given tips on how to be more effective in interviews to get my message out in a very short time without compromising my integrity or authenticity. That was very useful information.

While everyone in the meeting offered valuable insights, I left the room feeling that the opportunity was being viewed exclusively as a music-based one. No one there had everything figured out, but Brent in particular was adamant that there was much more to this than just music. The consensus from the music-industry people at the meeting was that this would be my 15 minutes of fame, and they suggested I leverage my music as much as possible while the attention lasted. With that in mind, they offered great commonsense advice.

So when this all began, it seemed logical that the biggest opportunities would present themselves within the traditional music industry, but the opposite has proven true. Very few radio stations played the song, and the national country music-video station didn't either, despite the millions of people who were watching the video and loving the tune.

When the radio and TV play did not happen, I was reminded that there is a prejudice as to how music gets heard in the traditional outlets when you don't have a label, a manager, a distribution company, a radio tracker, or a history of commercial success. Without those elements, "UBG" was just not considered a legitimate song. How could it be? It made people laugh, and was released by an unsigned artist no one saw coming, so surely it couldn't be any good . . . and after all, it was only on YouTube, right?

The fact is that had the number of people who have listened to "UBG" done so on a radio or a music-video channel, I'd be a millionaire. The fact that so many people are enjoying recorded music this way today is why the traditional music industry is dying.

I CONTINUED TO CONNECT WITH OTHER professionals who helped me in a number of ways as I adjusted to being in the spotlight and tried to figure out what to do with this newfound fame. For example, Alyson Queen was a PR person with our regional phone company at the time of "UBG," and I was very thankful to her for her advice about what to do in media interviews.

Shortly after the meeting of the minds, my father-in-law, Brent, introduced me to Phil Holmes, who works with an East Coast–based consulting company called Ambir Solutions. One of the things that make Ambir unique is the value they place on integrity and helping businesses succeed while caring about the customer and the greater good. It's no surprise that they were voted the number one company to work for in Atlantic Canada.

Phil gave me a few hours of his time one afternoon as we explored all the potential offers for work that might present themselves and which ones would be in line with who I was and who I might want to become. We also examined things that might look good on the surface, but that I should avoid. Before my meeting with Phil, I sat down with Brent so he and I could consider the essence of what I offered as a musician, speaker, and consumer advocate, and we developed a mission statement of "improving the world, one experience at a time." I decided to take responsibility for attempting to accomplish this mission with all things in my life, such as anytime I wrote or sang a song, gave a performance, presented at a speaking event, or just chatted with strangers I met.

So with this in mind, Phil and I took a look at my brand, what I stood for, and how I could fulfill my mission statement going forward. We mapped out what my career could look like in a best-case scenario and what I might need to do to accomplish those targets. By the end of it, we had a full whiteboard of possibilities, and he certainly had my gratitude and respect!

I found this to be one of the most positive experiences in those early days, because instead of focusing on what "UBG" could never be, we declared all the things *it could be* and just wrote them down. I'm happy to say that almost all of the things we listed that day have occurred or are in the process of happening as I write this.

Roughly a year after the release of "UBG," we were still trying to understand what the opportunity was and where the potential lay for my career. Brent introduced me to Tom McLellan and Ross Pierce, and for a time, we had a weekly strategy call to help me zero in on where all this was going.

Tom owns a company called Growth Click and is largely responsible for upgrading my business to "the cloud" and allowing me to offer a comprehensive online store. He also has a strong marketing mind and the ability to see the bigger picture in many situations. Ross is a lawyer from Saint John, New Brunswick, with a corporate background and a similar ability to offer good advice to those who need it. The four of us would enjoy regular conference calls, and I think those discussions were key in helping me understand what it is I could offer. They also kept me focused on the things I was passionate about, and this has been of greater help than I ever could have imagined.

I'M SOMEONE WHO'S BELIEVED IN GOAL SETTING for many years, but since all this happened in 2009, even I have been shocked by the power of deliberately writing down your goals. To me, it's one of those things you don't need to understand or even believe. Just do it and you'll be amazed by how things start to happen for you.

I'm often asked if I ever considered that "UBG" would be as successful as it was, and by now it should be obvious that I didn't. There is a lot of forgettable content on YouTube with millions of hits, so I was confident that if I made something that looked good, sounded good, and made people want to tell their friends about it, getting a million hits would be possible. But we just weren't prepared for what happened then—and in retrospect, I'm not sure how it could have been handled any better.

My goal of taking one year to achieve one million hits with all three videos combined was reached in just four days. By Friday of that first week, I had hit a million. By Sunday, the counter had hit two million. Getting a song listed for sale on iTunes wasn't as easy as one would think, and I'm sure we lost plenty of initial sales by not being prepared. I've been criticized for waiting until the video reached three million hits before being able to offer the song on iTunes, but the fact is that the video reached the three-million mark by the end of the second week.

By then, I had done more than 100 media interviews and received thousands of e-mails, and my tiny team had kept the website up and running; and to this day, I think we've responded to every offer for an interview, from bloggers to CNN to the smallest of newspapers. If we missed anyone, we're sorry, but we certainly did our level best. Managing all of it has been no small task, and I'm grateful to the people around me who made that all possible.

But even as I enjoyed my personal success, I never imagined what my little music project would end up doing to the large corporation that had originally abused my guitar—United Airlines.

♬ ♪ ♬ ♪ ♬

Chapter 7

UNITED'S REACTION AND INACTION

In the week following the release of the video, the pace at the house was a little hurried, to say the least. We had installed the two additional card tables in my tiny office, and just like my desk, they became buried under paper and folders. We were still waiting for the two-line phone to be connected, and my desktop computer became a gathering spot in the same way the radio drew a family together in the 1930s.

That little office became akin to a modern-day Norman Rockwell scene, with two or three people standing around a person reading e-mail messages at the computer. Because I was using Outlook Express to manage my e-mails at that time, my desktop was the sole destination for all those thousands of incoming messages.

I recall our "big crisis" that first week. Being aware that my story was embarrassing a multibillion-dollar corporation, we suspected that they would be using any and all means of stopping the groundswell of support for "UBG." At United's request, we had scheduled an appointment for a conference call with the company for that Friday. In the meantime, however, I continued to give interviews, and the YouTube numbers were well on their way to reaching one million. Clearly the airline would be working all the angles to counter this PR nightmare.

One afternoon in midweek we stood gathered around my office computer. With me were Julian, Brent, and Don, while Jill sat in the command chair reading e-mails. Without warning, my computer screen went blue. The only text appeared at the bottom, showing files quickly being scanned. Don, who reads a lot of Tom Clancy, quickly declared, "You're being cyber-attacked by United!" We all accepted that logic, and in the face of the Blue Screen of Death, we sprang into action.

When I say action, I mean mass panic. We had five people in a confined space, and our initial response to this attack was for everyone to simply switch places. Amid all this aimless shuffling, someone yelled, "What do we do?" So I made a move to pull the plug on my computer, a move that had worked in that Matthew Broderick movie *WarGames* from the '80s. It seemed like a slow-motion action scene when I felt someone slap my hand away, crying, *"Don't do it!"*

So as we watched my computer being destroyed from within, we decided to call an expert at a computer-repair shop for advice. People were shuffling papers wildly on the card tables as though a repair-guy business card might magically appear, but I think we ended up getting the number from the phone book. Julian worked the call as he relayed the situation to the expert on the phone, and from the command chair, he carefully delivered our instructions as though we were defusing a bomb. He'd listen to the person on the line and then give the order.

My memory of the event cannot be completely trusted because my recollection has Julian developing a British accent at this point and acquiring the voice of *Star Trek* captain Patrick Stewart. I put myself on standby to retrieve my wire cutters for the moment when Julian would call out the final instructions, "Now cut the blue wire," or something to that effect.

Instead, the instructions that came were to push the power button on the desktop tower, then hold it down. We did that, and the computer shut off. We all exhaled as the bomb was defused. Julian listened again and called out deliberately for us to turn the computer back on. We obeyed, and it started up without incident. Everything was as it should be, and we were back in business.

Apparently the Blue Screen of Death was just a computer glitch. Don recanted his declaration by saying, "Well, it could have been a cyber-attack." With the crisis averted, we shared a good laugh and carried on like nothing had happened.

SINCE JULY 2009, THE QUESTION that eventually comes up is: "What was United Airlines' reaction?"

With regard to me, the simple answer is that their reaction was consistent from the first day of this ordeal. They chose to do little or nothing and wait for it all to pass. In November 2008, it was the airline that shut down the communication about my issue and rebuffed any talk of compensation. I was told the matter was closed for good and that they would not respond to any further e-mails.

Almost eight months later, on Wednesday, July 8, a little more than one day after the release of the video, a United customer-service manager did phone the house hoping to speak with me about my guitar issue. By now, I was truly swamped with calls and inquiries for interviews and was busy traveling to TV stations to share the story so I missed the call. Brent, who was at the house to take it, arranged a conference call for that Friday afternoon. In the meantime, the video continued to pick up steam.

At the appointed time, we made the call to speak to the representative. He was very friendly and cordial, and he explained how even people at United's customer-service department in Chicago enjoyed the video's humor. As a joke, they had put a big "No" sign, similar to the one held up by Christine in the video, near the real Ms. Irlweg's desk. We all got a chuckle out of that. When we asked him, he said he was the only one on the line from United, but I suspected otherwise, because it sounded to me like we were on speakerphone. On our end, Brent and I were there, and we both spoke during the call.

One thing that stood out in that conversation was how very guarded United seemed in their choice of language. Instead of saying the airline was "sorry," the representative chose to say that what had happened was "regrettable." I've since been told by lawyers that those words are carefully chosen, because one statement implies sympathy and the other responsibility, the difference being that you can't sue someone for being sympathetic. I imagine the rep was coached as to what to say and how to communicate with me, but after some casual conversation, we got down to business.

When the airline's position became that what had happened was regrettable, the representative became empowered to offer the same $1,200 in United flight vouchers that I had requested back in November, plus an additional $1,200 in cash for my trouble. He was quick to point out that they weren't making this offer because I had a viral video on YouTube and added that they would make it to any customer.

I thanked him for the offer but refused it. To me, it seemed like my viral video was *precisely* the reason why we were talking on the phone and the only reason they were making that offer. Although they made no suggestion that accepting the compensation would require that I remove my video from YouTube, or that I not make the additional two remaining video installments, I felt that accepting it would weaken my credibility.

I explained to them that the company had closed the matter of compensation to me back in November, and I had accepted that and moved on. My goal of being compensated had evolved into a goal of sharing my story with as many people as were interested in hearing it. It also became an opportunity to improve conditions for all travelers, myself included. I couldn't accept compensation, because it was no longer on the table for discussion and this was now about something much bigger.

In saying this out loud, I considered all of my friends who had volunteered their time to make a difference with "UBG," and I wasn't about to diminish their contribution with a buyout. I was also aware that in the time it took United to make that offer, I had probably received 20 e-mails from around the world thanking me for the difference I was making in customer service and urging me not to accept the offer of compensation that many knew would come.

After only four days, I was witnessing a global wave of support for "UBG," and it became obvious that the video was a significant and evolving metaphor for change. It was more than just a story about a passenger and his guitar. I felt a sense of responsibility to finish the trilogy, and I won't deny that I was feeling the rush of the excitement in those early days. We all were: me, my family, my friends, and a mass of frustrated customers worldwide.

After declining the offer from United, I suggested that they instead find another customer inside their maze who was experiencing a situation similar to the one I had. I asked that they surprise that customer with a solution, and if United wanted to associate that customer's compensation with me, then I'd be happy to support that. The representative took that away to consider.

During the call, we also talked about the future. Brent and I explained that we fully intended to finish the trilogy. We explained that the second song was already written, so there was nothing that could change the outcome of that message. The video would be shot in the coming weeks, but I added that the third song had not yet been addressed and that United could have influence over how they were presented in it.

I suggested that if the airline were to make some kind of policy change that showed a positive shift for consumers, then I'd be happy to write about it in "United Breaks Guitars: Song Three" ("UBG3"). The representative seemed to listen and take notes to share with his team, and I was impressed by how very pleasant he was throughout the entire call. Meanwhile interest in the video continued to grow, and only a few hours later, we reached the goal of one million YouTube hits.

Within days of that call, what United chose to do instead was donate $3,000 in my name to the Thelonious

Monk Institute of Jazz, a nationally recognized institute in the United States that educates and develops some of tomorrow's best jazz musicians. That was a meaningful use of money, and I'm grateful to think that my experience might afford an opportunity to an aspiring musician who might not have had one otherwise.

However, it's worth mentioning that the choice of where to donate the money wasn't completely random. I was later told that a manager or executive of United also sat on the board of the Thelonious Monk Institute of Jazz. Nevertheless, the organization is solid, and the benefit to someone may be immeasurable. I have never discussed the matter of compensation with United since.

That isn't to say that I haven't kept in contact with the airline, however. Throughout the first few weeks, I had several conversations with their PR representative, Robin Urbanski, and actually met her in Chicago in September 2009.

In an ironic twist of fate, the week before I released "UBG," I had signed a contract to be part of a music delegation from Halifax attending the Chicago Irish festival in September. Each of the bands I'd be traveling with would be cross-promoting their own music with the province of Nova Scotia as part of the wider annual festival in Grant Park. I would be promoting my solo CD with my band and was excited about the opportunity.

Not long after the video had gone viral, though, I discovered that there was a third component to this Chicago trip. This music delegation from Nova Scotia was heading to Chicago to help our province promote the new direct route between Halifax and Chicago by . . . United Airlines. That was uncomfortable!

I'm sure the airline—and possibly even my client, who was working for Nova Scotia tourism—might have preferred that I not be part of that delegation after July 6, but I had a contract, and removing me from the bill would have been impeding my ability to earn a living. Even if they had paid my fee *not* to perform, the message would have been that United was denying me a career opportunity because they didn't like how I had shared my story about them. The potential reaction from "UBG" fans would have been too unpredictable at the time, so the idea of removing me from the roster was never discussed with me.

I was sensitive to the situation, however, and spoke to the woman who hired me. Whenever I perform, my goal is to put on an entertaining show for the audience but also to serve my client. She understood that I would have to play the "UBG" song, but asked that I only sing it once, at each of my three performances, and that I do it at the end of the show so as not to draw attention to it throughout the length of my set. It seemed like a fair compromise, so I agreed.

Rather than be seen as stirring the pot by flying with United direct from Halifax, I offered to take the long way there by going with Air Canada via Toronto. My client appreciated the gesture and agreed with the logic.

At that time, I was being recognized in airports and on planes constantly. For example, on a Sons of Maxwell trip not long after, Don sat beside a businessman who struck up a conversation about "this Dave Carroll guy from Halifax who did this amazing song" that was "changing customer service." When Don explained that he was my brother and that I was sitting in front of him, the gentleman was quick to reach over the seat to shake hands and ask for an autograph. This kind of reaction was common then and still occurs to this day.

So, when September came, we started our trip to Chicago with Air Canada by way of Toronto. When we landed at Pearson Airport and arrived at the connecting gate to Chicago, we discovered that *United Airlines* would be taking us the rest of the way. I had unknowingly bought a co-chair ticket, as the two airlines are part of the Star Alliance network. My effort to avoid United was in vain.

Chris Iannetti and I boarded the flight carrying our guitars. There were two flight attendants at the door to the plane, and their reaction told me that they recognized who I was but shared different opinions about my being there. The male flight attendant seemed happy to see me, while the woman . . . not so much.

Chris and I confirmed with them that we could bring our guitars on board if they fit in the overhead bin. Our seats were near the back of the plane, and I could see from the door that most of the bins in the rear were full. I did notice that just past business class there were empty bins above those seats, so we stowed them there on our way to the back of the plane.

Before we reached our assigned seats, the flight attendant chastised me over the PA with a message that said, "Ladies and gentleman, we ask that you put your personal belongings in the overhead bin above your own seat. I am now referring to the gentleman who put his guitar in the front of the aircraft. Would you please return and remove your guitar from the bin to be stowed in the belly of the plane?"

Chris and I waited for the aisle to clear and started to the front to collect our guitars. As we walked up the aisle, passengers who had recognized me were reacting like students in a high school detention room, anticipating a student-teacher confrontation (I would be the student). Some of the people were making an "Oooohhh" sound to imply impending doom, and I heard someone else say, "Dead man walking!"

I wasn't about to have an argument with a flight attendant on board an international flight, so we simply took our guitars down and met the flustered woman at the door. She was a bit testy and explained, never acknowledging Chris, that my guitar had used the overhead space belonging to passengers sitting below it and that their bags were now being unfairly stowed in the belly. She said we had taken too long to get our guitars down, and told us to turn around, put them back up, and retake our seats.

The male flight attendant gave me a wink and a grin as we turned around, while the sympathetic people in business class, who had been privy to the conversation, shook their heads as one of them exclaimed, "They just don't get it!" We took our seats, and the rest of the flight was uneventful.

While at the first of our three festival performances in Chicago, I had the pleasure of meeting Robin Urbanski from United Airlines in person. She came down to the show with her husband, and she and I exchanged a hug and had a great conversation. I liked her instantly and was reminded again how my issue with the airline was about policies, not individuals.

I had gotten frustrated in one of my earlier e-mails with Robin when she expressed concern that I might target Ms. Irlweg or her family in a negative rant. I had always spoken highly of Ms. Irlweg and actually made a viral video statement coming to her defense, so I was bothered by where this was coming from.

In my reply to Robin, I explained that nothing I had done would justify those concerns and that we should start focusing on the real issues. Since I was the CEO of my company, perhaps my time would be better spent in a meeting with the CEO of her company? Never expecting that to happen, Robin floored me when she replied, "How about a meeting with three VPs when you're in Chicago?"

So following that first performance, Robin confirmed that the meeting was scheduled for Monday morning at O'Hare with enough time built in for me to catch my flight home. When we met at the airport, she led me to a conference room within United's on-site headquarters, where I was introduced to the three senior vice presidents who represented Customer Contact Centers, Airport Operations, and System Operations Control.

(I had no idea when Robin left the room that morning that this would be our last meeting. Not long after, I was notified by her friend that she had become quite ill and would appreciate an e-mail from me. I was happy to connect with Robin again as friends do, and eventually she succumbed to her illness and died at a very young age. I'm relieved that I had never said anything unkind to her and that I was able to see the person she was through the policies she worked under, and most of all, I was grateful that I had made a new friend.)

In the boardroom I was feeling a bit outside my element, never having had an official executive meeting of any kind, let alone one with senior executives from one of the world's largest brands. Yes, I'm the CEO of my company, but I only have that title because my lawyer said that someone had to be CEO, and it might as well be me. The meeting didn't last long, but there I sat on one side of the table while three VPs sat across from me and explained what they did with the company, and welcomed my ideas on what I would like to see changed at United Airlines.

There was no suggestion that they would take my advice, but they listened, and it's worth noting that it was at this meeting that I heard an apology for the first time. All three apologized, actually, and while some might say that it came too late, it did make a difference to me. I appreciated the apology, and I think they appreciated the fact that I didn't run from the room to initiate a lawsuit when I heard it. Sometimes saying you're sorry is not only the right thing to do, but also the least expensive.

The VP of Customer Contact Centers talked about three areas where the airline was looking to improve. Management felt their customers would appreciate a friendlier staff, more comfortable passenger seats, and a decrease in flight delays. I agreed that those things would be worthy goals, but I was there because of a baggage issue. I took note that in the middle of the PR nightmare for their brand, the company was not addressing the root cause of their embarrassment. I wondered why, and I regret not asking that question. I think I was a little intimidated.

I explained that musicians have limited funds and that both they and their instruments need to arrive at their destinations together and in one piece. I therefore asked that a policy be adopted to allow guitar players to safely bring their instruments on board all United planes, or at least be allowed to gate-check them. Apparently that policy was already in place, but not all employees were aware of it. It was explained that with such a big company, educating all employees with respect to the policies takes time, but that they were making progress.

The VP of Operations explained that recent cost-cutting measures taken by the company had left some employees with more work, less money, and a reduced pension. He admitted that while those aren't ideal conditions, the employees were still well paid compared to "what's out there" and that management was dealing with some of those issues at the time. Bingo! Maybe many of these problems with United started and ended with how much their employees felt they were (or weren't) being valued?

One can relate to how the change in working conditions would be frustrating for employees, and it helps explain why both the flight attendants' and pilots' associations sent me letters of support and apologies for having been associated with my issue. While it doesn't excuse the mishandling of my guitar, it does help to explain why some employees might care less about their customers or the property they handle.

I think the simple answer is that the workers feel uncared for as employees! This frustration they feel would also be magnified by the fact that certain United executives were paid millions in bonuses for guiding the company through this difficult cost-cutting time. The VP didn't mention that perspective, but I've heard from plenty of United employees who feel ill treated by the alleged "wrongdoers" profiting on their loss.

Regarding the issue of guitars in the cabin, I did put in one request at the meeting. I said that if the company were making changes for the better, I would like to see a formal policy revision in writing. If they could e-mail me a copy of an old policy and a copy of the new-and-improved one, I would be happy to write about that in my final installment of the trilogy. That e-mail never came.

My final suggestion was that we resolve our disagreement on *The Oprah Winfrey Show.* With United being a longtime sponsor of the show and Oprah's interest in conflict resolution, I suggested that the airline could take the opportunity to turn things around by first laughing at themselves, and then telling the world about a change they were making that would be a win for consumers. They would actually have to *change* something, but they could show the world they have a sense of humor while doing it.

It seemed like a good idea to me. For me, I'd have the opportunity to maybe share my song "Now," which I really thought Oprah would love. No one else in the room seemed to agree with this idea, though. My concept was met with blank stares and what looked to me like an angry, nervous eye twitch from one of the VPs.

Still, the meeting ended cordially, and I was invited to take a tour of the behind-the-scenes operation at O'Hare, which included a trip up to the control tower to watch a few takeoffs and landings. The whole morning was a unique and enlightening experience.

Occasionally I've kept in contact with the VP of Customer Contact Centers and have acted as an advocate for affected passengers. I've helped a few guitar players with broken instruments get satisfaction, and I've even branched out to assist a golfer in getting compensation for lost clubs by connecting him directly with my contact person. Each time I've been thanked by United for taking the time to be a good ombudsman.

Since United Airlines merged with Continental Airlines, I took Whoopi Goldberg's advice and spoke to the company about their use of my video for training purposes. When I was a guest on ABC's *The View* in January 2010, the show aired a response from United that acknowledged that the airline was using my video as a training tool. Whoopi asked me if they had paid a license fee for that use, which they had not. She thought they should, and I agreed.

SINCE THE VIDEO'S RELEASE, several well-known companies have licensed the use of "UBG" to show their employees an example of the risks of poor customer service. These companies volunteered to pay a license fee for that right.

In early 2011, I therefore asked United for their reasoning behind telling the world they were using "UBG" to improve customer service, making their company more profitable, yet not offering me the same license fee as other companies. As I write this, United has agreed to a fair license fee, and they have joined the ranks of other respected brands as paying customers of mine.

The *principle* of being paid the license fee was what mattered most to me, and I decided to give the money from United, aside from legal fees, away. I gave some to Scott Ferguson as a thank-you for all the work he donated recording, mixing, and mastering the songs. Scott purchased a new piece of recording equipment that is allowing him to make the music from his many client projects sound even better.

Beyond that, I was able to use the license-fee money to help out an Indiana woman and a Florida man who had special medical needs. With the former, I was able to cover her financial commitment to acquire a special service dog to assist her in coping with her daily challenges with muscular dystrophy. The money I gave both of them made their lives a little easier. I also donated money to cover the cost of two operations for children with cleft palates in developing-world countries through an organization called Smile Train ($250 each). And finally, there was just enough money left over to cover the cost for the first two months of a multiyear commitment to sponsor a second World Vision child from Africa—a boy this time. My wife and I had sponsored a girl years ago.

Since "UBG" had been enjoyed around the world, by both friends and strangers, I felt it only appropriate that the money from that license fee be distributed along the same lines, and I can't express how good it felt to do it.

♬ ♪ ♬ ♪ ♬

Chapter 8

WHAT TO DO FOR AN ENCORE: "UBG SONG TWO"

Given the mayhem of July 2009, it was lucky for me that the second song in the trilogy had already been written. "United Breaks Guitars: Song Two" ("UBG2") was born in March 2009 and took a fresh look at my experience both stylistically and lyrically. Part of my goal with the project was to write about my story from three different perspectives to keep it interesting to listeners and challenging for me as a songwriter.

With that in mind, I went from telling the facts in the first song to exploring my relationship with Ms. Irlweg in "UBG2." I also changed musical gears and went from a pure country sound to what I've termed "German Oom-Pa Pop" (with apologies, and serious doubts that this name will catch on . . . or ever be used again).

While the first song laid out my story as a series of things that happened to me, Song Two was an appeal to United to stop the fighting and change their ways. The song speaks to the airline's flawed policies that were preventing an otherwise beautiful friendship from developing between Ms. Irlweg and me. Thus, the video reveals some of the things she and I might do as best buddies if it weren't for those policies keeping us apart—things like romantic picnics and three-legged races.

This ongoing United experience contains an endless series of firsts for me, and with "UBG2," I had written my first song calling for a tuba. Actually, it *screamed* tuba, and I've learned to go with my gut when that happens. I was inspired by the old A&W commercials where the Root Bear mascot would travel the world on foot, gathering followers who were compelled to walk in step behind him to the hokey tuba melody of the A&W song. It was like a slower, groovier, urban-conga-line thing.

Once again I called on my friends to help with the recording and welcomed a few new faces to the project. Scott Ferguson again supplied the studio and drums at Ferguson Music Productions. Ian Sherwood played the sax and clarinet. Kim Dunn joined us on piano and tuba solo. I had tapped out the tuba bass line on a keyboard using a tuba synth, and Kim played the tuba solo when he recorded his parts.

We deliberately made that tuba solo a little over-the-top and unbelievable. In fact, we were so successful that after we released the video, in defense of his craft, Alan Baer, the principal tuba player with the New York Philharmonic, jokingly demanded that we never do that again and offered his services in the future where tuba was required.

EACH VIDEO HAS GREAT MEMORIES attached to it, but in many ways, "UBG2" was my favorite. First of all, there was a lot of excitement, as everyone in Halifax was following the story closely, and people around the world were curious as to how I'd follow up "UBG." Earlier that month, the Halifax *Chronicle Herald* newspaper made me an honored guest in the annual Natal Day parade, so I brought my two "baggage handler" friends from the video along with me.

While Charlie, Phil, and I sat in a convertible and followed the parade route, I was surprised by the warm reception we received from the thousands of people cheering, smiling, and laughing at what we'd accomplished. Apparently I was the *Herald*'s second choice when NHL star Sidney Crosby wasn't available. Not a bad act to follow!

For our video, we wanted to show people coming together in solidarity for "UBG2," not unlike the happy following of people behind the A&W Root Bear. But instead of a message selling fast food, our video would promote nonconfrontation, and to help achieve that, I decided that Ms. Irlweg should surprise us with her virtuosity on tuba and lead us all through a positive transformation.

The audio track has a gang of singers joining in the chorus, and the rhythm is designed to make you tap your foot and shake your booty. To support the song, the video would need many feet and a fair bit of booty. Chris Pauley took on the job of finding extras and posted a Facebook page where people could express interest in coming. He would contact them to give the location and date when the time was right, and chose this system because simply putting out a cattle call would have been too risky.

There was a real possibility a thousand people might have shown up, and we had no license, insurance, or security to block streets or handle a large crowd. Chris invited the first 100 people who volunteered to take part, and the day before the shoot, we asked them to show up with a white T-shirt and hat to the Station 41 fire hall. I also enlisted the support of family, including my dad, Jill, and even Flynn for a short cameo, but my 88-year-old grandmother was a tough sell. In her British accent, sounding like Queen Elizabeth herself, she justified her hesitancy, saying, "I like to keep a low profile, David." I pressed her, and she finally relented.

THE FILM CREW WAS MORE ROBUST for this video, but again, most everyone volunteered. We had camera assistants and a lighting guy. We had a makeup person and an official photographer to capture behind-the-scenes stills that day. We had an art director, in addition to Barb Richard, who was back working on props, and someone was assigned to keep all the extras in one place. My mom, Sharon, was enlisted to manage "craft services" (aka food), and we had a cargo van and limousine available for some important scenes. It felt like a much bigger deal, but we still had only one day and needed to make the most of it. We shot the whole video in 15 hours, and if you watch, you'll notice how many costume and scene changes there are. It was an ambitious day, and Steve and Lara from Curve Productions pulled it all together so capably with the help of their team.

This time, Steve, Lara, and I met in advance of the shoot to storyboard the video and came up with a very cool shot to close out the song. It would require a high-angle perspective, so we considered a helicopter—but we didn't know anyone who owned one that we could borrow, and we certainly didn't have the budget to rent one.

A helicopter would have attracted too much attention in Waverley anyway. Instead, I called MacFarlands rentals in Halifax from the number in the phone book and asked for the day rate on their tallest scissor lift. The person told me, "The 60-footer would run you about $500." He asked what I needed it for. I told him I was a musician shooting a music video about how United Airlines had broken my guitar, and he interrupted, "'United Breaks Guitars'? We'll donate it!" We were set for our big finish.

In "UBG," one of the shots that people enjoyed was the one with my guitar lying broken on the tarmac, akin to a dead body. A crime-scene investigator consoles me as I sit grieving beside it, and when he takes away the guitar, a chalk outline of my dead Taylor is revealed.

We wanted to reintroduce that chalk-outline idea to close out "UBG2." The notion was to place the camera and crew on the extended scissor lift in the grassy area behind Station 41. From above, they would direct and arrange all the extras in white T-shirts and hats into the shape of a large, perfectly intact guitar. Some of the other characters and I would stand in a small circle inside the guitar to form its sound hole, and we'd all sing and dance to the song until it ended.

At that point, someone would signal the last 12 people at the end, standing in the shape of the guitar's neck, to move downward in sync and make it appear as though the guitar's neck was breaking (to look just like the chalk outline from "UBG"). Someone would then signal everyone to scatter out of the camera's frame and leave me alone to place my guitar on the grass and walk off myself. Finally, a white cargo van with UNITED written across the top would enter the frame and drive over the guitar two or three more times to end the video.

We filmed "UBG2" on a hot and sunny day in mid-August, and the big guitar scene was the last outdoor shot of the day. All the extras had been extremely patient, aside from being sun drenched and a little tired. However, we were losing light by the minute, so we had only one take at this scene. I was also concerned about my grandmother getting heatstroke, as she had been doing great all day, but was starting to feel the strain.

The shot was clearly explained to everyone by handheld megaphone and then rehearsed. It worked great. They called "Action," and everyone danced and sang as directed. The song ended, the neck broke, and everyone scattered to leave me alone to place the prop guitar on the grass and walk off.

When I stood up, though, there were still two people in the frame who didn't get the memo about exiting gracefully: they were my grandmother and the lady holding her up! In the video, you can see my reaction of trying to whisk her off the field as quickly as possible and out of the shot. What you don't hear is her chastising me in her strongest English accent, "Where are we going?! No one told me anything!"

We also took the opportunity with this second video to say good-bye to the Three Amigos. After "UBG," I received several e-mail and interview questions asking, "Why the Mexicans?" Some people were concerned I was diminishing Mexican people in some way, but the simple truth was that the Three Amigos singing mariachi-style harmonies fit the part and seemed funny to me. Another reason is that *Fun in Acapulco* is my favorite Elvis Presley movie, and in it, he sings with mariachi guys. So I figured, if it worked for the King, why not give it a whirl myself?

When I raised the Mexican sensitivity issue, Chris Iannetti had the idea to change the Amigos to something else for "UBG2," and the logical choice seemed to be German guys in lederhosen. Chris and Mike were both available and into that, but Jimmy Inch (that irreverent Amigo #3) was on vacation in Newfoundland and couldn't make the shoot. Those were big shoes to fill, but I put out the offer of German Guy #3 to my friend Ian Sherwood, another East Coast musician and songwriting talent, who jumped right in and took ownership of that role. We had our three German characters.

If it's true that music brings people together, then "UBG2" definitely did on that day. The smiles you see on everyone's faces are genuine. The vibe was positive, and there was a sense of possibility in the air—that we were following through on something important. It was a long, hard day, but it flew by and we managed to say all we wanted with that video.

We showed Ms. Irlweg as a fun-loving person saddled with a tough job. We showed the bad baggage handlers as a minority and not representative of all United employees. We addressed the issue of CEO bonuses in the face of company-wide cutbacks. Most important, though, we showed that any company's brand is nothing more than the sum of the stories being told about it . . . and that those stories are shared by individual customers like any of us. What was the big lesson for companies? No customer is expendable, and we are all part of a bigger whole.

When we released the video, it didn't take off as we hoped it might. It has done exceeding well by YouTube standards, sitting at nearly 1.5 million hits, but it shows how guaranteeing a viral video today is next to impossible. "UBG" has always been the workhorse of the three, and any original is always hard to beat with sequels. Still, reaction to "UBG2" was powerful, and reviews were overwhelmingly positive.

With "UBG2," I continued to get support from a range of interesting people, as well as interview requests from major media. It was still exciting, never knowing who might call next, and I had embraced the fact that, at any time, there were no limitations on who or what might be around the next turn. While Joe Rogan from Ultimate Fighting Championship was in my corner applauding my fighting technique with United, a Buddhist monk was also supporting me for the nonconfrontational aspect of the video. Wildly different audiences were seeing the video from different perspectives, and each day was a real adventure.

Not long after the release of "UBG2," I got a call from a casting director in Halifax. We have a medium-size film industry in town, and it's not uncommon for feature films to be shot here. I had recognized the casting director's name from conversations with Lara Cassidy, but we had never met. When this woman called my cell phone and said, "We're casting for a movie being shot in Halifax starring Olympia Dukakis," I thought, *With all the crazy things that have been happening to me lately, why <u>shouldn't</u> I be called to be in a movie with Oscar winner Olympia Dukakis?*

I waited for the director to ask for my availability, but then she continued, "And we're wondering if your grandmother is available. We loved her work in Video Two!" I was stunned. My 88-year-old grandmother,

Doreen "I prefer to keep a low profile" Daley, had stolen my thunder!

When I raced to her home to share the good news, once again she was a tough sell. "You want me to be in the Olympics . . . why on earth—?"

But I interrupted her to explain: "No, Grandma, an Olympia Dukakis movie. She's an award-winning actress."

She finally came around, and said, "Well, if you'd like me to . . . all right, then."

So my grandmother ended up landing the role in a hospital scene of an Olympia Dukakis movie as the Sleeping Lady in Bed Two. She lay in a hospital bed opening and closing her eyes on command and made $160 for the trouble, money she later donated to charity. When she got home after her shoot, she said they had treated her very well and that she was retiring from acting, reminding me once again, "I prefer to keep a low profile, David."

Not long after that, my grandmother was diagnosed with terminal lung cancer and died in March 2011, peacefully in her sleep, at my parents' home. I'll always be grateful to have such a vibrant and living memory of her in that video to show my son and look back upon myself. Of all the positive ripples caused by my videos, that one is a personal favorite.

Just weeks before she died, I wrote a song for my grandmother, attempting to sum up her life in under five minutes, and presented the recording to her in my home studio. When faced with the death of loved ones, we often consider doing something special for them but wait too long. Following through on writing and sharing that song before it was too late was one of the wisest decisions I've ever made. Her reaction was moving. For the first time, I saw my grandmother cry, and through her tears she gave me a profoundly humble thank-you and said, "No one's ever written a song for me."

In an effort to share a little of the person she was, I am including the lyrics and recording of this song, "God Save Doreen," as part of the book. The recording is the same one my grandmother heard that day in my office, complete with little imperfections, but I share it as another example of how effective music can be in transmitting a positive message and reaching others. I hope you enjoy meeting her in this small way—she was such a larger-than-life influence on me.

♫ ♪ ♫ ♪ ♫

Chapter 9

THE BIG FINALE: "UBG SONG THREE"

Things continued at a frenetic pace throughout the fall of 2009, and I still hadn't written the third and final song in the trilogy. I had already far surpassed one million hits in one year, but the other component of my goal was writing about my experience from three unique and entertaining perspectives.

Our first "UBG" song was country and stuck to the facts of the incident. The second one was a "German Oom-Pa Pop" song exploring the customer's relationship with all the Ms. Irlwegs of the world and their poor company policies. How, then, should I approach the last installment to bring closure to the story, and could I give United a chance to vindicate itself?

When I met with the three United VPs in Chicago in September 2009, I asked them to identify a policy that had been changed since "UBG." I explained that if they could show me in writing what the policy had been, and what the policy had been changed to, then I would be happy to share their good news in Song Three. That never happened, so in late November 2009, I wrote the final song in the trilogy, called "United Breaks Guitars: Song Three" ("UBG3"), without any input from United Airlines.

The wish list of objectives with this song was long. Every good story has a beginning, middle, and end, so this last segment had to not only say something new, but also sum up what had happened *and* shine a light on the future. Musically it had to be unique, and when it came time to do the video, I wanted to bring together as many of the characters as possible to say good-bye, similar to the way the *Seinfeld* TV series had been wrapped up.

I had considered going in the direction of a love song or power ballad, akin to the kind of song that ended every high school dance I'd attended (in which case, Ms. Irlweg and I would meet under the glitter ball and live happily ever after, or until the song ended . . . whichever came first). But after further consideration, I decided this song needed to be fun and energetic, so a happy, upbeat approach seemed to be the ticket. The answer came to me in no time at all: bluegrass!

Bluegrass has a great energy behind it and is a highly skilled form of music. It may not have mainstream popularity, but there are communities of fans around the world who love it, including unbelievable players who spend years practicing the craft simply for their own enjoyment.

Bluegrass is roots music, so the lyrics tend to have relevance in the lives of everyday people, and the music itself is like a conversation where several instruments get an opportunity to speak, taking turns playing the melody and improvising around it. I think the entire "UBG" story does the same thing, being relevant and relatable to all and providing a platform from which others can share their voices. Therefore, energetically and metaphorically, bluegrass was a perfect choice.

The message of "UBG3" was simple. While the first two songs examined a relatable experience from my perspective, "UBG3" takes on more of a spokesperson role for all customers. The thousands of e-mails I received told me that I wasn't alone in being frustrated by poor customer service, so I use a gang of other voices in the chorus to reflect our common frustration and delivered this warning to United:

You say that you're changin', and I hope you do,
'Cause if you don't, then who'd fly with you?

In "UBG3," I reflected on what happened before and after the incident in 2008, and because this song would be my last word on the topic, I warned United that I represented just the tip of the iceberg of growing customer frustration. Whereas I might be done writing songs about it, like a good bluegrass tune, another player may step forward with a fresh voice if required.

I wanted the music to be authentic for this last tune, and because performing good bluegrass is beyond my own ability, I needed to bring in some outside help. By the time I began writing the third song, I was convinced anything was possible, so I asked the question "Who is a well-known bluegrass heavy hitter who could add credibility to this song?" The only name that came to my mind was dobro player Jerry Douglas. (A *dobro* is a resonator guitar commonly heard in bluegrass music.)

Jerry Douglas is a Grammy winner, has played with Alison Krauss and Union Station for years, and stands out in the company of the best dobro players in the world. I decided to ask Jerry to take part and e-mailed his manager, whose address I got from a website, explaining who I was and what I was doing. I heard back shortly afterward that Jerry would gladly take part and donate his services, like everyone else. It probably didn't hurt that in the demo I sent, before the section that would become a dobro solo, I had introduced Jerry's name in the song.

United needs to understand, their customers ain't helpless.
And while they sit and ponder that, let's hear from Jerry Douglas.

I was thrilled that Jerry would take part, but now I'd need world-class fiddle and mandolin parts to accompany Jerry's dobro. That choice proved easy, and I picked up the phone and called Ray Legere from New Brunswick. Ray is one of those multi-instrumentalists who is better on fiddle, flat-top guitar, and mandolin than most people could ever hope to be on any one instrument. He had played on two Sons of Maxwell recordings, and I recall fondly the one show he did with us in Timmins, Ontario, earlier in our career.

Ray is highly respected in bluegrass circles, and after a show in Timmins, while we were sitting in a restaurant, fans of Ray's who had driven 60 miles in a snowstorm to see him walked in with a big upright bass guitar and a video camera. Ray didn't know them, but they asked if he wouldn't mind getting his fiddle out so that they could videotape the experience of playing together. Rock musicians probably wouldn't have done it, but Ray obliged, and they jammed for a while right there in the restaurant. That speaks to the friendly nature of the music and those who play it.

Upright bass was the only choice for "UBG3," so I called on Halifax's Jamie Gatti once again and was glad he could do it. I would play rhythm guitar, and Scott Ferguson would lay down some drums and record those parts at his studio. I had the band lined up and the song was written, so we were off to the races.

We laid down the rhythm parts first (drums, bass, and acoustic guitar), followed by Ray's mandolin and fiddle parts, leaving room for Jerry to record his dobro at his own studio in Nashville. The finished product showcases some world-class playing, and as far as pure musicianship goes, "UBG3" is my favorite. As a songwriter, I'm honored that something I wrote is supported by that level of playing, with the likes of Jerry and Ray donating their time and talent to the cause.

WITH THE SONG RECORDED, it was time to look at shooting the video. By now it was December, and with everyone's schedule, we'd have to wait until January before we'd have the chance. Shooting outdoors in winter was not an option, so we had to secure a new location.

We didn't have far to go from the fire hall, though, as we were welcomed by the Waverley Legion just down the street. In Canada, following World War I, the Royal Canadian Legion created a network of establishments across the country for veterans. Most communities in Canada have a Legion branch, and they are active in each community, offering their halls for meetings, weddings, and other functions. The Waverley Legion hall would do just fine for "UBG3."

We needed to consider the next evolution of the Three Amigos as a concept, and I decided that "bearded hillbillies" seemed most appropriate. I put the call out to Mike, Chris, and Jimmy, the original Three Amigos, to transform themselves into the Three Billies. All were on board. I imagined that hillbillies don't really grow their beards, but rather keep them hung by the door, like hats on hooks, to be worn when they leave the house. We included that gag in the video, and it's one of my favorite parts.

Karen and Paula were back as flight attendants. Charlie and Phil were once again committed as the baggage handlers. I made a call to Christine Buiteman and confirmed her for Ms. Irlweg's final farewell. We needed extras once again to represent the people and had a few dozen sign up for that, including Tim Feswick (producer of four Sons of Maxwell recordings). Curve Productions once again assembled a great crew, and we were ready! We had a location, a cast, and a crew, so we decided to meet on a snowy Saturday in January and bid farewell to the creative side of "United Breaks Guitars."

On shoot day, we needed to improvise a bit more than expected. Nova Scotia had been hit with storm, and Mike, who lived two hours away, was unable to leave his driveway because of the snow. We were disappointed in Mike that he didn't plan for all contingencies and have a snowmobile or dogsled on standby, but he's since redeemed himself with a ten-inch, full-color tattoo of the broken guitar from "UBG" on his forearm. Nevertheless, we needed another hillbilly, so we gave Tim Feswick his dream shot. Tim went from being an extra to a featured hillbilly in one day, and although it wasn't a speaking role, he was thrilled with his meteoric rise as an actor!

Once again we enjoyed a great day shooting the video and had fun involving so many people. Christine is a trained Irish dancer, and we'd talked for years about her dancing to some of our Celtic tunes at a show sometime. It seemed only fitting that Christine, in her role as Ms. Irlweg, should have the final say in the trilogy with a random introduction of a Riverdance-style tap-dance flurry . . . and, once again, put a point on the fact that customer-service agents are people with hidden depths, just like the rest of us.

When we finished the final scene, someone shouted, "That's a series wrap," and people moved around the room, shaking hands and hugging each other, with a sense of both accomplishment and regret. I had done what I had set out to do in just over a year and greatly exceeded my expectations in the process, but I was sad to say good-bye to something I had enjoyed so much.

Lara still had to arrange to get footage of Jerry Douglas in Nashville playing to the song and then edit all of that into a finished video, so that took us into February. I was touring in Ireland during the second half of the month, so the launch of the video had to wait until I returned home on March 1. While I had been away in Ireland, though, Jill and Brent had been busy organizing an innovative launch plan that would allow people across the world to tune in and watch the video together with us for the first time in Halifax.

We booked space at a spot called the Hub for a traditional release party, with drinks and snacks for roughly 50 people. The plan was for me to introduce the video and answer some questions before posting it to YouTube, but the innovative part included a live video stream from our event to registered online guests. It was an excellent way to promote the launch and acknowledge that

"UBG" had a global audience. As a result, instead of 50 people at the release, I had more than 2,500 guests from more than 20 countries join the party, and by the time I got home that night, "UBG3" had been named the Bluegrass Song of the Month by the São Paulo Bluegrass Music Association in Brazil.

While the fan favorite tends to be the first song and video, I've enjoyed watching the debate from other fans standing behind either the second or the third in the series. Without question, though, there is a synergy between the three. The fact that each video tells an important part of the story strengthens the message in the other two, and today "UBG3" is approaching 500,000 hits. Regardless of the numbers, I'm proud of all three efforts and the work we accomplished to produce them.

There's no question that everyone involved was enjoying the splash we had made with the videos, but the ripples were beginning to be felt on a variety of shores.

♬ ♪ ♬ ♪ ♬

Part III

SOCIAL MEDIA AND OUR CONNECTION TO EACH OTHER

Chapter 10

ARE YOU STATISTICALLY INSIGNIFICANT?

So far, I have summed up United Airlines' reaction to me personally and my interaction with them since my fateful flight through Chicago's O'Hare Airport with the band in March 2008. Since then, I learned many lessons about the mysterious world of social media and customer service, and one of the most revealing concepts I have run into is that of *statistical insignificance*. I believe these two words should never be used in business, because no customer wants to feel statistically insignificant. I will explain this further within this chapter, but first, let me share a short summary of the buzz the "UBG" trilogy has created in the social-media and customer-service landscape. This discussion will put me and my role into better context, explaining how, over the past few years, I moved from musician to advocate.

Let me start off by saying that I'm not the only one who feels that United really missed the boat in responding to the videos. Since "UBG" went viral, countless authors, researchers, and presenters have invested significant time evaluating how United reacted as a brand. *Empowered* by Josh Bernoff and Ted Schadler and

Real-Time Marketing and PR by David Meerman Scott are two good sources. *Wired and Dangerous* by Chip R. Bell and John R. Patterson is another. Of course, Harvard's case study is highly regarded, and Allison Soule's University of North Carolina–Chapel Hill master's thesis, called "Fighting the Social Media Wildfire," gives a thorough academic examination of the "UBG" phenomenon.

The general consensus is that United grossly mishandled the affair from start to finish. They were criticized for ending all discussions on my claim. Their employees were not empowered to take responsibility and make decisions that could have prevented this from escalating. When the video went viral, their strategy was to communicate with me off-line or through traditional media releases while the conversation was being fueled online. Simple things like saying "I'm sorry" took months to happen.

Before YouTube, this story would have struggled to see the light of day. In 2009, though, social media had afforded me the ability to share it with a mass audience. United was completely ill equipped to handle a customer-service nightmare in the age of social media. The airline should have had a social-media strategy to engage the interested communities and partake in the online discussion. Instead, they monopolized the conversation with traditional press releases that attempted to downplay the issue or deflect attention. Today's consumers are intelligent and tech savvy and won't settle for one-sided comments in old-fashioned media statements. Consumers want to be heard!

United had also applied limited resources to Twitter and Facebook, and both were fundamental contributors to the success of "UBG." At a company as big as United Airlines, why were they caught so unprepared? How could they have done better, and what should other companies do when faced with similar situations themselves? That is what so many people have been trying to determine since 2009. United Airlines' reaction to my video has fueled as much interest in "UBG" as anything I may have done, and it's their own reaction to the crisis that has allowed the video to become a benchmark in customer service and social media for years to come.

It wasn't until after releasing "UBG" that I discovered that the customer-service industry in North America is a $120-billion-a-year business. That surprised me, but it explained why there was so much interest in the video from the customer-service world. I was hearing from presenters and professors everywhere telling me that they were including my story as an example of the dangers of poor service. I soon discovered how my story had gone far beyond just the airline industry—but it was another airline experience that revealed a fundamental issue fueling the video's success.

In September 2009, I was invited to Capitol Hill in Washington, D.C., to take part in a hearing in support of an Airline Passenger Bill of Rights sponsored by Senator Barbara Boxer. A private citizen named Kate Hanni had the unfortunate experience of being on an airport tarmac stranded in a plane for many hours. Without adequate food, water, and bathroom supplies, Kate and her fellow passengers endured an awful experience, and later, realizing that her experience was not an isolated incident, she felt compelled to see that it would never happen again. Kate has since worked with politicians and action groups to enact legislation to eliminate those occurrences, and she felt that my participation, from a property perspective, could have an impact.

I was the lone Canadian giving testimony that day and the only one speaking about luggage issues specifically; and, once again, I was struck by the irony of how a broken guitar had led me to this place. There we were—me, the band, and Brent—in a congressional hearing room to give testimony in an attempt to change U.S. law. The bill has since been passed, and stricter laws are now in place to heavily penalize airlines for serious delays. I'm honored to think that I contributed in some small way to that end; but at the very least, we broke a little new ground that day, as I'm told we were the first to ever sing testimony inside those walls.

Also at the hearing that day was a former airline CEO whom Kate enlisted to voice support for the bill. He was an excellent speaker, clearly very intelligent and well-spoken, but I had difficulty understanding whose side he was on. Although she wasn't in the room at the time of his speech, Senator Boxer agreed with me because she criticized his comments later that morning, at which point the CEO interrupted her to say, "Senator, I'm on your side," to which she replied, "Then why was I told otherwise?"

The CEO's analysis did not appear customer service–centric, but rather it focused on the challenges airlines face in today's business environment. He acknowledged that these unfortunate incidents do happen occasionally, but by and large, almost all planes leave the ground in a reasonable time. In his expert opinion, the constraints called for in the bill were too onerous on the airlines and would cause more harm than good. While agreeing that it would be unfortunate to be one of those unlucky few trapped inside planes during excessive delays, he said that such examples were "statistically insignificant" when measured against the thousands of flights where that doesn't occur.

I couldn't believe what I was hearing. This person had been in charge of a company handling millions of customers each year, and he was implying that the experiences of those affected by horrible customer service are insignificant as long as they are statistically rare! If this gentleman were in college, his analysis might have gotten an *A* in stats class, but he would have earned a solid *F* in customer service.

From what I can see and feel, the concept of statistical insignificance has to be one of the most destructive ideas that certain companies employ when it comes to customer service. The basic premise is that the goal should be to get it mostly right, most of the time, so that the number of customer-service failures are so few compared to the number of uneventful interactions that they are statistically insignificant and therefore not worth worrying about.

This implies that there is some measurable portion of your customer base that doesn't matter; that you can absorb the fallout of leaving a bad impression on some of the people who keep you in business. I believe that this is antiquated thinking, and suggest that any company who shares this philosophy today is shortsighted and doomed in the long run.

Before social media, news of a bad experience was often restricted to word of mouth, and I've read that one person's bad experience would be shared with 14 people. Companies could use what I call a "hide and ride" policy of doing nothing and waiting for negative feedback to blow over. Not anymore! In my case, I shared my story only twice; using one Facebook message and one e-mail to my e-mail list. Four days later, one million people were telling their friends about my story, and United was caught flat-footed in an outdated culture that embraces statistical insignificance.

When the focus becomes meeting targets for the majority and having no plan for those who fall through the cracks, your company is living on borrowed time. Today every individual consumer has a voice, and while statistics are helpful to gauge the effectiveness of your service, they should only be used to reveal what needs fixing, not to applaud yourself for what went right. If stats were a fire-detection system, companies that embrace the "statistical insignificance" culture would congratulate each other if they discovered a blaze in only a small part of their building. The rest of us would pick up the phone and call the fire department.

During the early months of "UBG," United, on more than one occasion, issued media releases reminding us that 99.6 percent of their bags arrive on time and without incident. Rather than acknowledge what wasn't working, they promoted the good side of the equation. Considering that the airline flies tens of millions of passengers each year, that amounts to many thousands of baggage incidents.

Is that statistically insignificant? To a mathematician it may be, but if you run an airline or have anything to do with customer service, seeing those numbers should leave you in a cold sweat and hunched crying in the fetal position. It will take just a few years for United to amass *one million* customers who have had delayed or damaged baggage. How many people will hear about

I took an incredible trip to Emerald Lake, Alberta, not long before the fateful one to Nebraska. Had I known my Taylor was soon to be broken, I would not have been so happy.

This is the only existing still photograph that I know of from the making of the first "United Breaks Guitars" video (taken with my cell phone). None of us could imagine what was coming.

Screen shot of Charlie, me, and Phil from the first "UBG" video. We're on the tarmac, otherwise known as the parking lot of our local fire hall.

The crime-scene-style chalk outline of my poor broken guitar was just a simple, fun idea we used in the first video, but it has since resonated with frustrated travelers around the world.

The icon that opens doors for me; it has become the perfect image for my company, Big Break Enterprises Inc. (Trademark of Dave Carroll)

A screen shot from the very emotional funeral scene in "UBG," with us in mourning for my broken guitar. I still find this sequence difficult to watch.

My tour of the Taylor Guitar factory in El Cajon, California, was an amazing day. I got to meet and take home a new friend—my Taylor 810ce—plus a second guitar, too . . . both compliments of the company!

With all the buzz in 2009, editorial cartoonist Bruce MacKinnon had fun with the story, too—published September 24.

Suited up for my next flight and looking ahead with great optimism.

Me hanging with the boys—Ian, Chris, and Mike—in "UBG2."

These videos were truly the result of the support of so many good people, like Todd!

Having a blast watching some playback from "UBG2" for the first time.

Ms. Irlweg and I are enjoying a three-legged race, with our three German friends from "UBG2" cheering us on. Christine played the part of Ms. Irlweg perfectly in all three videos.

The Germans on the move in "UBG2"! Not since *Snow White* has there been such a merry band of lederhosen-clad travelers.

A romantic picnic with Ms. Irlweg.

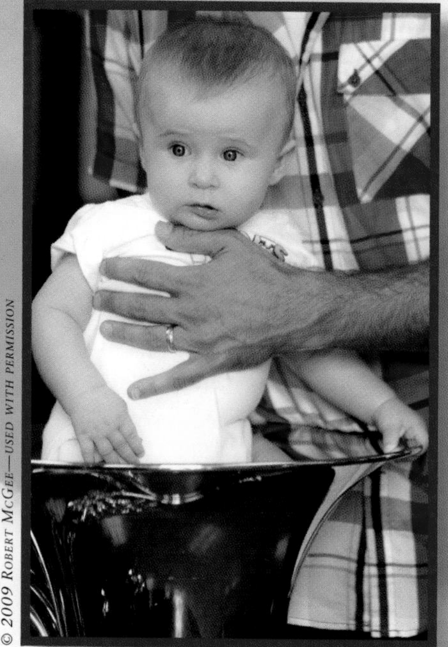

No, the tuba did not give birth to Ms. Irlweg's and my love child. This photo is of my son, Flynn, taken on the day of the "UBG2" shoot.

The 60-foot scissor lift in action shooting our epic scene in "UBG2."

Here Lara is sitting and watching the filming through the monitor while her sister, Anne Marie, leads the cast in dance.

My grandmother Doreen Daley, launching her acting career at age 88.

The crowd of "UBG2" was in fine form. My grandmother is on the far right, and my dad and Julian are on the far left.

A great metaphor for the broken promise between the company and the customer, from the "UBG2" video.

Here my wife, Jill, and I are at the Consumers' Choice Awards gala in Halifax, Nova Scotia, where I accepted their inaugural "Man of the Year Award" in December 2010.

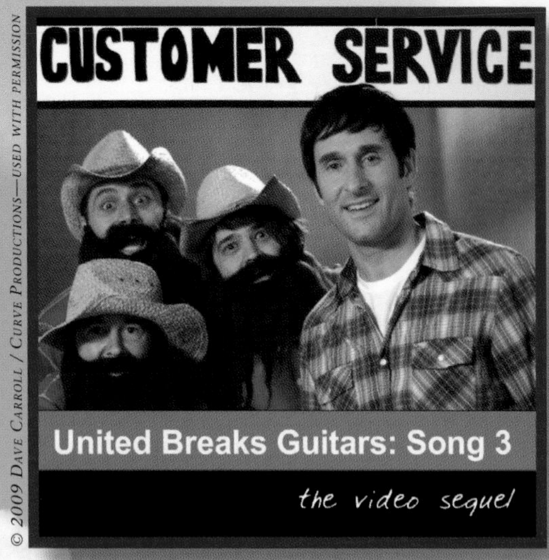

Rounding out the trilogy, the Three Billies and I kick off "UBG3" in this shot, taken from the video.

Me and the Three Billies "leaving nothing on the field" in "UBG3."

For no apparent reason, we broke with continuity and included Julian as "Transient Billy 1" in "UBG3." There were no other transients.

Talented illustrator Liisa Sorsa of Timmins, Ontario, makes a living capturing the essence of corporate messages at special events through her company: **thinklinkgraphics.com**.

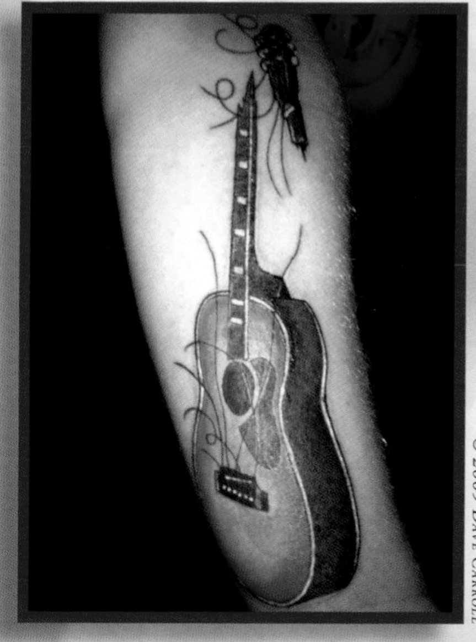

Mike Hiltz displays his own unique (and permanent!) commitment to my plight.

All in the family: Don, Dad, me, and Mom.
I've just got to get me another one of those velvet shirts.

Here we are, me and Don, Sons of Maxwell, on picture day.

these bad experiences? How many will decide to get creative and tell others through social media? Getting it mostly right is nothing to boast about in this case, and anyone with an understanding of the power of social media knows the significance of those numbers.

I believe that companies need to hold themselves to a higher standard—a standard no different from the one I hold for myself and that many other companies also embrace. When performing, I don't strive to play 95 percent of my songs well. I expect to nail all of them. I'm far from perfect, but when I do make mistakes, they come as a surprise, and I do my best to see that they don't happen again. It's about constantly trying to improve your level of service and being very concerned about giving good value to every single customer.

Today's healthiest companies understand that good customer service is a requirement for success. They shoot to get it right every time knowing that there will be breakdowns along the way, but the difference is that their customer-service model has room to recover. Their philosophy starts with the fact that all customers deserve a positive experience—not most of them, but *every one* of them. The fact that even a small percentage of a customer base is unsatisfied is antithetical to a customer-centered business, and it shows in how they recover from a bad experience.

It's worth noting that conflicts are resolved more quickly for companies that reject the statistical-insignificance model, for two reasons:

First, they recognize the value in the satisfaction of the affected customer and are quick to remedy a bad situation. In solving a problem, you have an opportunity to strengthen loyalty, and learn more about his or her preferences so you can better serve in the future.

In fact, studies show that customers who have a problem and get that problem solved actually like the company better than those who never had a problem—a phenomenon known as the *service recovery paradox.* Once a customer-service issue occurs, companies have a choice—they can approach dealing with their customer as a problem or as an opportunity—and the outcome depends on what they choose.

The second reason has to do with the customer, who is more likely to accept a resolution when he or she feels respected and valued. A conflict requires two opposing forces to collide. When an angry customer is met by indifference from a company, that individual responds angrily. A customer-service representative who is encouraged and empowered to find a resolution, however, does much to reduce a conflict before it gets out of hand. Like attracts like, and most often, customers will react in the same way they are treated.

The companies that wish to be profitable a decade from now will adopt this approach to customer care because they understand that there is no part of that pie that can be marginalized without risking a viral backlash. In my case, one bad customer-service experience was heard around the world. As more dissatisfied customers find creative ways to use social media, companies subscribing to a philosophy that accepts the notion of statistical insignificance will be compelled to care more or become a statistic of their own, adding their names to the growing list of companies that no longer exist.

♬ ♪ ♬ ♪ ♬

Chapter 11

SOCIAL MEDIA AS A GAME CHANGER FOR BUSINESS

After I had written my fateful e-mail to Ms. Irlweg, declaring that I would capture my experience in a trilogy of music, I started doing some research. I noticed that YouTube was hosting plenty of poor-quality and forgettable videos with incredible numbers of hits behind them.

Although the quality didn't inspire me, the fact that there were so many videos with large YouTube counts convinced me that if others could get there, then so could I. Attaining a million views had to be possible, but I wanted to do it without being hateful or having to film myself in a dress riding a bicycle off my garage roof. I decided to go with a high-brow approach instead and asked my friends to be mariachi singers!

Rather than simply trying to get to one million, I committed myself to creating quality content that I hoped would be so entertaining that people would not only tell their friends but return to watch it more themselves. If I could do that, then surely I could reach a million views or more. I wanted to have what I'll call *meaningful numbers,* so my social-media strategy needed to be a little different.

Asking the right questions when you face any challenge is the road to an answer, so I asked this fundamental question before engaging in a social-media campaign: "Can I make something that looks good, sounds good, and makes people want to tell their friends about it?" In my case, the answer was yes. Thanks to my friends, who volunteered their time and expertise, my $150 video features a well-produced soundtrack and movie-quality camera work. The content is strong by design, and as a result, people have returned to watch the videos countless times and told their friends to watch.

As I write this, "UBG" has exceeded 11.5 million views. Is my success affecting how others view social media? It is, absolutely. People are inspired by the fact that I found an inexpensive yet effective way to hold the attention of others for over four minutes in order to share my message. Just as I knew that reaching a million YouTube views was possible by virtue of the fact that others had done so before me, today millions of other people are now inspired knowing they can do what I did with their own creativity, authenticity, and integrity.

Every day, people like me are waking up to the fact that what they have to say matters, and that they have the tools to present their message in a way that stands out. In the eyes of many, the bar has been raised by "UBG," and any limits on what was thought to be attainable by one person's message have been replaced with limitless possibilities. Without a doubt, some incredibly effective videos are going to be made on the heels of what happened with "United Breaks Guitars," and I think that's very cool!

However, it is the effect the video is having in the business world that really makes "UBG" unique. It's a rare thing when something on YouTube goes viral, but even rarer when it starts affecting the profitability of a large company. When that company and other businesses worldwide consider changing how they view customers because of a viral video, then that becomes news. For that reason, I'd like to focus the rest of this chapter on my take on why social media and "United Breaks Guitars" aligned to send ripples around the business world, and how this is good for consumers.

CORPORATIONS AND AD AGENCIES have always known that to be successful, you need to be where your customers are. If sports fans are your company's demographic, then you'd be wise to spend some money advertising at a sports arena (like Chicago's United Center, for instance). If you're appealing to fans of rock music, you might sponsor a rock festival. *Social media* has recently become a buzz phrase in business as more companies wake up to the fact that if their customers are immersed in social media, then that's where they also need to be.

In spring 2011, I attended a conference in Austin, Texas, known as South by Southwest (SXSW), which includes both a music-industry portion and a social media–focused event called "SXSW Interactive." I was one of the 18,000 delegates at the 2011 SXSW Interactive. I was engaged by RightNow Technologies, a U.S. software company that develops customer relationship management (CRM) software, to help them draw attention to one of their initiatives.

We did a guerrilla performance at the conference center that week—a short performance in a random spot where lots of other people might be. You make do with what you have in the unlikeliest of places and simply perform, which suits my philosophy perfectly. I recall that we were standing in the crowded hallway of the convention center when someone with RightNow suggested I break out my Taylor and ride the escalator singing "United Breaks Guitars." I was a little uncomfortable initially, but it ended up working out great.

The RightNow Technologies team had hired a camera crew to cover the conference and had also employed several attractive models to hand out flyers promoting a big event they had organized. So together, we started on the third floor and rode the long convention-center escalators to the bottom. I was positioned in front of the camera crew and surrounded by the RightNow team and models as they enthusiastically clapped and joined in my impromptu version of "UBG" that appeared to be instantly recognized by about 1,500 people in just three minutes. Because SXSW is attended by people heavily involved in social media, most of the 18,000 delegates would have known about "UBG." As I played my first-ever escalator set, there were people scrambling to take pictures on their cell phones or pointing and saying, "Look, it's the United guy."

What struck me at SXSW wasn't just the size of the event, but how many big brands were present in the city that week. It was obvious that these companies were there to be visible and, most of all, relevant. They didn't just have signage posted on walls. Some hosted cool parties, while others set up booths in hallways offering food or battery-charging stations for devices. They were there to be seen and to be of value. These brands were spending a lot of money in the hopes of standing out and anchoring themselves to a contingent of social-media influencers—people who have lots of online followers who listen to what they have to say. I can't say what return they got on their investment, but companies that were present at SXSW *get* social media, and as time goes on, all businesses will target customers using it to some degree. It's inevitable.

Social media is not only a way to advertise, but more important, it has become the way to learn what your customers want and what they're saying about you; and caring about what they're saying has never been more important. I've heard it said that in the age of social media, your brand is nothing more than the sum of the conversations about it. To a large degree I think that's a fair statement, and most business professionals and social-media gurus would agree that the "UBG" videos, or others like them, have answered the question "Is social media relevant to your business?" I'm not sure that all companies are moving to embrace social media, though, and the question is: *Why not?*

I personally think that the answer has to do with two issues: fear and ignorance. Learning and implementing something new can be a daunting task. It's difficult for small businesses, already overworked with day-to-day responsibilities, to add another to-do to their list. In large organizations with many employees who are grouped in business silos and divisions, any embracing of a new culture or practice can be painfully slow. Another issue involves understanding rapidly evolving technology; many executives and small-business owners simply don't understand what social media is, let alone how to embrace it.

In light of "UBG," many businesspeople wonder, "Why should I invest in social media so that I can help angry customers share their bad experiences with others?" They view social media as a funnel where you attempt to manage a deluge of unfounded customer-service complaints. No wonder these companies fear it. Who would want to enter into that kind of atmosphere?

Social media is much more than that, however, and I believe that embracing it is the only answer. If online communities are forming to speak negatively about your company, then the answer isn't to ignore them or issue a press-release statement attempting to deflect attention to something else. The answer is to enter the conversation and possibly even lead the discussion to a resolution.

Social media is about communication, and today listening has never been more important. The good news is that listening is where we do our best learning. It's been said that we have two ears and one mouth for good reason, and that maxim would apply here. If someone complains about your company, and a growing number of people are supporting that message, it's clear there is something wrong with your brand. Wouldn't you want to learn what that is so you could fix it? Wouldn't you want to hear about it first, before it spins out of control? Social media allows you to do that, and the truth is that customers today are going to enlist social media to share their stories whether you invest in it not. The reality is that these customers also have the ability to reach an immense audience.

If you can appreciate that we're all customers to somebody, and that a customer is a person who simply makes a conscious decision to spend his or her limited time or money with you, then why are so many companies missing a golden opportunity to develop stronger ties with their clientele? Knowing and caring about what your customers think about you is fundamental to the health of a business, but many companies have forgotten that.

For musicians, our fans are our customers, and I'm always grateful to those who choose to come see me play. I have a belief that if you care about the customers you have, they will come back again another time and bring their friends. That's why after a gig, I engage with people, either to simply chat or to ask for feedback on the performance.

The result is that people at my shows usually get what they expect and more, and then tell others about their experience. If I fail to deliver the goods in some way, then by welcoming instant feedback, I have the chance to make things right immediately and retain a fan who I hope will continue to be an evangelist for my music. I've built my career on referrals, and like all musicians, I depend on the fans I meet tonight to share their good experience with friends tomorrow.

The online environment is just like that. By embracing social media, companies have an opportunity to engage directly with their customers. It sends the message that you value your customers' opinion and want to retain their business. By listening to what they want and need, and adjusting your business to deliver that, you don't just accomplish a sale. You become relevant to your customer. In other words, you matter to them, and with all the competition and choice available today, you want to be relevant to the ones who keep you in business.

Now that I'm not just a musician but also a public speaker, I've been enjoying this new role of attending conferences, and the opportunity to listen to the powerful messages of other speakers. For example, it was fascinating to present at a Columbia University conference on branding and innovation along with Barack Obama's social-media strategist and many other experts. Even more surprising to me was when more than half of these other high-profile speakers referenced me and "UBG" in their speeches that day!

I also really enjoyed participating in a social-media conference in California in 2010, where I got to listen to Scott Monty of Ford relate an aspect of his company's social-media strategy. Scott explained that in the past when an automaker wanted to release a new car, they might do some independent research to develop what they determined was a winning product. They would allocate a large marketing budget to advertise it and launch it; then spend more time and resources selling the merits of their vehicle; and, finally, hope for the best. When Scott spoke, he explained that Ford was interested in launching their Fiesta line and that they felt their engineers had done an excellent job in creating a great car within its class. Ford thought outside the box, however, and decided to do something innovative with the Fiesta launch.

They decided to embrace social media and use it to test-market the vehicle. Before launching the Fiesta, they gave dozens of these new cars to digitally connected people across America to experience for a time. The only instructions were to "create one themed video a month; otherwise, just do what you'd normally do." There were no restrictions on what they could say or how to say it.

Those who fear social media might view this as a risk: *What if they don't like it, or what if they might tell people negative things we don't want to promote?*

My mom has an innate ability to turn a phrase, and on occasion, she's been known to say, "You can't polish a turd." In other words, if you sell crap, then today's savvy customers will know it and tell each other. Companies that rely on polish for inferior products should fear social media. But for those that care about quality and go to great lengths to ensure it, I say there is minimal risk to embracing social media. Ford recognized these risks and took care to make certain they test-marketed a car that had no weaknesses that they could see. They viewed social media as an opportunity, and it paid off on several fronts.

It turned out that the Ford engineers *had* done an excellent job, and customers loved their Fiestas. The focus group not only told Ford what they thought, but they shared their impressions with everyone they knew, online and in person. As a result, Ford received 10,000 advance orders for the Fiesta based on word of mouth, and the company's initial marketing budget for launch was a fraction of the traditional cost.

Not everything was perfect according to the consumer feedback, however, and because Ford was able to learn this information before it went to market, they were able to reengineer small aspects and make the Fiesta even more appealing. In other words, Ford crowdsourced some of the design work of a car, for free, and took the advice of the very people who would reward them with the purchase of a relevant product later.

But what about the companies without the same level of confidence that Ford has? What about those that are freaked out by social media and worried about vigilantes like me? I don't personally think of myself as a vigilante, but I know some other people have used that term.

Are people like me a threat? It depends on who you ask. If you put the question to United Airlines and Taylor Guitars, you might get different answers. Consider that both companies had an opportunity to take something bad that happened to me and turn it into a profit for their company. Each had an opportunity to share their story with millions of "UBG" onlookers and profit from the fact that it's your *story* that people buy, not necessarily what you sell. The reaction and the degree to which each company embraced social media to share their stories left Taylor and United with drastically different experiences.

The airline seemed to resent the attention and stayed relatively silent, hoping to ride it out with no real social-media policy in play. Taylor, on the other hand, realizing they had potential customers looking at them for the first time, made a YouTube video featuring Bob Taylor referencing "UBG." While the company didn't dwell on my video and allow "UBG" to hijack their brand, they did use it as a platform to introduce the Taylor philosophy of making guitars, and they even went a step further.

Bob used his video to inform all air passengers traveling with guitars of what our rights are according to the Transportation Security Administration (TSA), and where we can find those regulations online. In other words, Bob Taylor welcomed the attention of the video, harnessed social media to promote Taylor's story, and made his video relevant by providing useful information to the public, specifically anyone who might be traveling with any make of guitar. Bob was leading a relevant online conversation in the space where everyone was already gathering, and as a result, his video went viral, too.

What makes "UBG" so important in the business world is that United's and Taylor's reactions directly affected their bottom line in some way. *BBC News* announced that for a time in 2009, "UBG" had dropped the market capitalization of United Airlines by 10 percent, or $180 million. That kind of effect sent ripples of fear throughout corporate boardrooms around the world as certain executives were heard asking, "How do we prevent a 'Dave Carroll' from happening to us?"

It doesn't have to be all bad news, though. In 2011, Taylor announced they had their best year ever, with sales up 25 percent from their previous best year ever (all of this during a recession and with a discretionary item). I don't believe all of those losses or gains can be attributed to my video, but "UBG" certainly had some impact, and I think that it was directly related to each company's response to the opportunity afforded by social media.

From now on, companies like Taylor and Ford will come to depend on social media to develop market-winning products because they know that customers influence each other more than any ad campaign ever can. Using social media to be where their customers are only makes sense. As a bonus, a well-made product will require less service, and some of that $120 billion spent each year on customer service can be invested elsewhere or taken as profit. Social media is an integral part of that.

Here is another case in point. In March 2010, I was invited to Boston by the Chubb Group of Insurance Companies to draw attention to their booth at one of the largest insurance trade shows in the world. Chubb is a $13-billion-a-year company, and all the big names in the industry were at the event, vying for attention and the chance to engage customers. What interested Chubb about my story was the fact that my video affected the market value of one of the world's major brands. Among other questions, they asked risk managers and others for ideas on how companies could protect themselves against such social-media perils as a viral video. The implications of this are huge.

Can you imagine if insurance policies existed to protect companies against negative viral videos, and companies were buying them? To be insurable, they would have to sustain a certain level of quality and service with their products. No company would insure your home against fire if it knew you were storing gasoline in the basement. Likewise, a claim for the lost business associated with the reputational damage caused by a negative viral video might not be accepted if you failed to take responsibility for breaking a guitar in view of passengers.

All companies with this type of insurance would be forced to operate within insurable standards to the benefit of all, and the risk of a viral backlash would be minimized because a higher level of customer service would be required. It appears that the fear and economic impact of one customer's voice sent ripples through the world's business community, and the fact that this type of risk management is even being seriously contemplated is at least in part because of "UBG." To me, that is just incredible.

If a company is going online to engage customers about their products, they will need to be able to speak intelligently on all issues or have access to meaningful answers. It's possible that PR departments will give way to a Social Media Relations (SMR) department as the focus on two-way communication between all stakeholders becomes the way of the future and the ticket to staying relevant in customers' eyes.

The big difference between a traditional PR department and a newer-style SMR department is that the latter will proactively reach out to customers for feedback and lead conversations within online communities to stay relevant. Moving from monologue to dialogue will mean the PR department will need to understand all aspects of a company's product line and be able to communicate with both the average consumer and the CEO. That will require both an understanding of social media and cooperation from all departments in a streamlined organization. As a result, the Social Media Relations department could become one of the most important divisions in any company.

Part of the legacy of "UBG" is that it has inspired consumers and companies alike to think innovatively with regard to social media. At speaking events I am often told by audience members, from executives to consumers, that "UBG" has led to fundamental changes in the relationship between businesses and their customers. While frustrated consumers have realized there is a creative way for each of us to be heard, companies of all sizes have gotten past the fear factor surrounding social media and broadened the scope of what it can mean to their bottom line.

I used a social-media platform to share a message, and I reached millions in the process. Because I was extremely successful, others continue to study the story in university textbooks and refer to it in business presentations around the world. Even a first-grade class in Pennsylvania followed me online to illustrate the power of one person, and they sent me a recording of them singing "UBG." Each time someone watches the video or hears the story, it has the potential to change the way he or she thinks about social media. Helping set the stage for what those people think next is where the power of "UBG" really lies.

♫ ♪ ♫ ♪ ♫

Chapter 12

MY LESSONS LEARNED: WE ARE ALL CONNECTED

In August 2011, I made my first visit to Australia to both speak and perform in Melbourne and Sydney. When you consider that it takes 30 hours to get there from Halifax, that you cross the international date line, and that you catapult 13 hours into the future when you arrive, you're left with the distinct impression that you are far away from home.

While I was there, however, I had an amazing experience that reminded me again of how small the world really is. On my final day in Sydney, I decided to visit the famous Bondi Beach, so I jumped in a taxi and asked the cabbie to take me there. The driver was a big man with a strong Eastern European accent. We started talking, and it turned out he was a Romanian political refugee who had served in the military during the time of Nicolae Ceauşescu.

As we talked about world politics and the recent social movements happening everywhere, he randomly remarked in his thick Romanian accent, "You know, like that song 'United, United' . . ." and he continued speaking.

I interrupted him and asked, "What did you just say?"

He apologized and explained, "My friend, you probably wouldn't know, but there is a man from Canada who wrote a song about United Airlines."

I stopped him, exclaiming, "I'm that guy!"

He looked at me in disbelief, likely mirroring the look that was on *my* face, and immediately pulled the cab over to the curb so he could turn to fully face me. He was laughing and screaming, "I can't believe it! I can't believe it! The United man is in my cab. I will call my wife, and she will not believe it!"

He told me how he had enjoyed following the story and the trilogy and that he talked about it often to his customers. We chatted a bit more before he continued on to Bondi Beach, where we shook hands and said goodbye. Today, the other side of the world is right next door.

THIS UNIVERSAL TRUTH CONTINUES TO raise a question that I have tried to answer in virtually all of the hundreds of media interviews I've done in the past two years. The question invariably comes up as to why I think "UBG" was so successful. In my early days of the experience, the nearest I had come to understanding what made the video unique was that it resonated with people. The fact that others could relate to my story made them able to enjoy my response as if it were their own. A victory for me was a victory for everyone who has ever flown, and a victory for customers everywhere who have felt disempowered by giant companies performing badly.

There is some truth to this, I'm sure, but now that I have gained some perspective, I find I can look below the first few layers of this experience. And it is there that I've discovered what I feel is the real reason why "UBG" was so successful. It has to do with *being connected.* But before delving into that further, let me dispel some misconceptions about "UBG" by explaining what it was *not.*

The success of "UBG" was not about anger or confrontation. Despite the fact that there was no anger in my approach to the videos, I have received countless e-mail messages from people congratulating me for "kicking the big dog's behind." Without question, some people are attracted to watching a fight, and many of us enjoy seeing a little guy do well against a "big dog." And virtually all of the interest from the media with regard to my story is also founded on this notion. The media loves to play up a confrontation, using headlines like "Disgruntled Customer Takes Revenge."

So while the media's presentation of my story as a form of customer vigilante justice has fueled interest in "UBG," I personally have never embraced that notion nor agreed with it. My vision of a vigilante is a sweaty, angry, and irrational troublemaker who only thinks as far ahead as the next wrongdoer he's going to punish. I don't recall ever being "that guy" during this experience.

While vigilantes set out to break the rules to exact their vengeance, what I did was different. Rather than set out to break rules, I simply rejected United's policy and aimed to *change* the rules by exercising my rights as a consumer. Which approach you choose to follow will lead to wildly different outcomes, I believe.

Admittedly there was plenty of anger and frustration when I was inside the United Airlines customer-service maze, but from the time I sat down to write the first song until today, I haven't been in a fighting frame of mind. That has made all the difference. From my perspective, my goal was never to get revenge, but rather to compel United to take responsibility and to see that hurting their customers is damaging to their own business. I wanted them to see that there aren't two sides to consumer stories like mine, just one: the right side. While revenge is a negative and angry emotion, my approach was anything but vengeful.

Very early in the process, I started looking below the surface reasons as to why the video attracted so much attention, and in doing so, I zeroed in on the reaction other people have after watching the video. I started looking for common threads that made it so popular. I began to go beyond the idea that it merely resonated with people and started thinking about how incredible it is that something is even *able* to resonate with so many different people in the first place.

What is it about our makeup as human beings that can explain how individuals in China, Germany, India, and Brazil shared happily in my experience when they don't speak my language and, culturally, we couldn't be more diverse?

It was then that I had an epiphany. The video resonated with everyone because all people long for connections and positive experiences. It goes without saying that we are attracted to things that make us feel good and avoid things that cause us grief. We join clubs to be around like-minded others. We belong to online communities for the same reason. Musicians depend on fans to come together and watch their live performances. These actions of coming together really aren't random decisions, though. I see them more as instincts we're inclined to follow.

I believe that at a deep level, we are all programmed with a desire to experience connection with other people. We want that connection and are being drawn to it, at times without even realizing it. Whereas some of our passions and interests can be shared in small communities or like-minded groups, there are certain ideas that exceed the confines of a specific interest group; concepts that everyone can embrace as *our own.*

In my case, like a puzzle piece finding the right fit for itself, people around the world discovered an effortless connection with my story because "United Breaks Guitars" promotes a universal message that we all want and deserve mutual respect, and caring for things that we value.

A former CBS television executive I met summed it up best when he explained that "UBG" was a "unique expression of a universal truth." I loved the sound of that when I heard it, because it encapsulated what the video is all about. When we experience a universal truth, it just feels right and is easy to accept. There's no selling involved. The essence of the message is immediately and wholly understood and seems to come to *us*—it doesn't feel like it takes work to find it.

When you're faced with a universal truth, there's no confrontation or argument, because there is no other side to defend against. It's something everyone can agree with, and a confrontation requires at least one opposing side. Combining catchy lyrics, upbeat music, and fun images made for a powerful communications tool, but the essence of connection in my message was universal in its appeal. That was the key!

"UBG" has been heralded as a classic David-and-Goliath story because United Airlines is a giant corporation and I'm just one customer who suffered a bad experience with them. In actuality, there hasn't been any confrontation between us since the release of the video.

Although the experience may have been somewhat unpleasant for United, even they have reluctantly accepted the universal truth in my message. To their credit, they eventually apologized, offered compensation that exceeded what I had asked for in 2008, and have been pleasant in all my dealings with them since the video was released. The problem was that they offered those things only *after* I actually followed through on my promise and had a viral video on YouTube. By then it was too late.

United's reaction supports this idea that the essence of "UBG" is a universal truth. For them to take a confrontational approach against me after the video's release would have been to deny that I was clearly wronged, and that denial would have infuriated the public even further. The groundswell of negative opinion would have been far more damaging to their brand, because they'd be defending a side that no one else believed even existed. What would be the point in defending a weak position that would only hurt you more in the long run?

So, if it's true that we all long for connections and good experiences, and the video allowed us to experience a universal truth, then maybe the real reason for its popularity was something other than the attraction of watching a fight.

Here's where I think this gets really interesting. If you accept that people long to experience connections with others, the bigger question then becomes: *Why do they long to do that?* Could you say that things like my video actually *form* those connections? I don't think so. I don't believe that my video created bonds between people where none had existed before. The answer has to be bigger than that, and here is what I've come to understand.

We don't just long for connection. I believe that all people are connected with each other as a natural state of being and that this bond doesn't need to be fabricated. It already exists and always has. We *are* connected, and we long to feel more of that natural connection with each other.

This isn't a new concept, and I certainly didn't invent it. This idea is a fundamental principle in most major religions—as well as New Age thought—and now the nature of social media is proving it to us daily. Examples such as my video only serve to remind us of this undeniable fact.

You will often hear that Facebook, and social media in general, is thriving because it connects us with other people, but is that really true? A high school friendship that is reestablished via Facebook isn't *created* on that platform—it is only experienced there if people choose to use this avenue to reconnect. In other words, that original friendship already existed, but Facebook is thriving because it allows us to *experience* our connectedness to other human beings in a meaningful way.

In the same sense, antique-car lovers don't love old automobiles because they belong to a car club. They already love old cars, and they join these clubs because they can enjoy the experience even more when they are around other people who love them, too.

Likewise, social media allows us to satisfy an urge to share our experiences with others and affords us the opportunity to experience what others wish to share with us. To say that Facebook is a source of our connection, I think, is wrong and misses the mark. Facebook and all the other social-media platforms simply let us experience our connectedness, and this subtle difference carries massive implications.

THE TRUTH IS, NO ONE WANTS TO feel alone or separate. When relationships break up, we often turn to songs that remind us that others have felt the same way. In a similar sense, a roller coaster is best enjoyed with friends because sitting in pairs or groups on the ride enhances everyone's experience as a shared one.

On the other extreme, suicide may be explained in a variety of ways, but in many instances, it's ultimately the result of people feeling utterly disconnected from life around them. We want to know and feel a connection with others, and sharing experiences is a way to achieve that. Understanding this concept and striving for it is what I think we're born to do.

It's ironic that with all the technological opportunities we have to connect with people today, we are, at the same time, challenged to experience connectedness. Over the years, we have been encouraged and manipulated to see ourselves as separate from one another on superficial levels. In today's hustle-and-bustle world, we spend the majority of our time trying to attend to our own needs quickly—and often at the expense of others, because we have been conditioned to believe that *dog-eat-dog* is the only mantra for the masses.

Through media and advertising, we are bombarded daily by messages and suggestions about how different we are from one another; that our differences exceed our commonalities; and that we need to fear certain others or worry about not being enough like some. There is a definite "us and them" perspective in how we have been conditioned to communicate with and relate to one another, and this dualistic mentality is how we tend to live each day and approach conflict resolution. It is also extremely limiting.

The news media is particularly guilty of this. Turn on the TV any evening and almost every story will be designed to share someone else's misfortune so graphically that this person's experience feels like your own. If there isn't enough death and destruction close to home each day, news organizations, knowing that audiences find these stories and images hard to ignore, will locate a story halfway around the world of a bus that overturned, killing 17! Regardless of where you live, there are both buses and embankments, so these stories are sure to engage you to imagine yourself, or your loved ones, in a similar accident.

While the goal of the news should be to share meaningful information, too often the objective is simply to hold our attention through the next commercial break. Nothing does that as easily as good old-fashioned fear and anger. Advertisers pay broadcasters for commercial time. Fear and anger hold our attention and increase viewership, and ad rates increase with a larger audience. There's quick profit in promoting fear and anger, and that's why most of the news is bad. Of course there's the nightly exception of that one closing feel-good story about a panda being born at the San Diego Zoo, but notice how that story is placed at the end of the show, where it doesn't matter if you come back from the next commercial break or not. The show's over!

SELLING FEAR IS BY NO MEANS restricted to the media. Advertising companies make millions packaging an antidote to fear, and by bottling and selling us exclusivity. Whether it be promoting antiperspirant to ensure you're not lumped into the sweaty-and-stinky category, or selling the latest exercise program that promises to make you look like the fitness models in their commercials, we are pushed and prodded daily in one direction or another.

The profits for the individuals doing the pushing are related to how effective they are at *separating* people. Making us believe that we are separate from one another and offering us "a way in" or "a way out" is the fundamental principle in many businesses today. It's about creating demand for what only *you* have to sell by creating two sides: the haves and have-nots.

When this becomes the lens through which you see the world, it becomes a problem, though, because you constantly see yourself on one side of everything or the other, and being on the correct side requires constant vigilance and action. That's not only expensive, but it's exhausting.

Life doesn't have to unfold that way, however. Changing our perspective can be the difference between a life of chaos and one of harmony. Conflict arises when we focus on the differences between each other, while those of us who go looking first for common ground more often find harmony and experience less confrontation. Individuals and businesses that accept these realities and work hard to build true experiences, connections, and relationships will undoubtedly have more success.

So once it sinks in that all people share an inherent connection to one another, and that longing to experience that connection forms the basis for many of our choices, everyone would be wise to take note. If we are really connected at the deepest level, then that would explain why it feels good to help others (because we're really helping ourselves). It can also account for why it's so frustrating to be treated badly and, if you think about it, why it feels so unpleasant to hurt someone else (because we're really only hurting ourselves when we do). The impact of this inherent truth can be felt not only on a personal basis, but also in business.

♫ ♪ ♫ ♪ ♫

Chapter 13

LESSONS FOR BUSINESS: LISTEN TO THE POWER OF ONE

What does this idea that we are all connected mean to those in business? Plenty, that's what! In business circles, many competitors have engaged in a "race to the bottom" in terms of what they charge, believing that the most competitive price gets the sale. The sales approach is to show a target audience *what* you sell and find the price point the customer will pay for that product or service. If the product or service is not selling, or the competition is strong, the answer becomes to drop the price. Other times you see ads for products that focus on the wide array of features, but neglect to mention the inspiration behind the product.

I won't suggest that pricing isn't an important part of a business plan or that directing attention to the best features of your product isn't relevant, but I would suggest that customers don't just choose to buy *what* you make. They are buying the "maker"—the *story* behind the company that developed that product. Therefore, explaining and presenting who you are as a company is becoming just as important as what you sell, if not more so.

So why is so much time and energy being invested in showing product differentiation instead of sharing who the company is and their unique story? To me that defines an opportunity lost.

So many businesses operate on the premise that you focus on select people who like a specific thing, and you sell them a product that appeals to their niche. The music industry works that way. Country record labels sign country artists to make country music to sell to country fans. Think about all the people in the world they are excluding, though, by focusing so specifically on the product of country music and the narrow demographic of country fans.

I posed the question "What would happen if I wrote a song that cast a wider net and was more about the message than the genre used to present it?" Everyone I know has more than one style of music in their collection, so I've asked, why do I need to consistently write in only one genre? Wouldn't it be possible for fans of other genres to expand their tastes if the message is right?

"United Breaks Guitars" is much more country than I would normally produce, but my goal was to write in that genre because it helped amplify the message. Rather than target just guitar players with my song, or only fans of one musical genre, I set out to share my story with anyone in the world who wanted to hear it, and I used the country style to help tell it. I asked listeners to "buy into me" through my music. That's a world apart from how record labels approach their business. For me, the results speak for themselves, and from a business perspective, there is profit in this kind of philosophy.

I received a great e-mail months after launching the first video, and the message started like this: "Dave, I have to tell you that I hate country music." Not exactly the warm and fuzzy start to the fan e-mail I expected this to be. The writer shocked me, though, in his next sentence when he said, "But I love what you're doing, I love the way you're doing it, and I love your story. That's why I'm buying everything you've ever recorded. I'm buying your T-shirts and DVDs, and I'll come see you live if you're ever in my neck of the woods."

If I had set out to sell this man my song ("what I do"), he would have walked away after hearing the first four bars of "UBG," and I would have lost 99 cents from the download. Effortlessly, though, he was sold on my story ("who I am") and purchased $300 in product and music he'd never heard, because he had faith that he'd like it. He didn't just buy the digital downloads, either. He bought the physical CDs as a memento of his experience with the video. By casting a wide net with a message that speaks to everyone, I found a customer who cut through the superficial layer of "what I do" and who bought "who I am" instead.

If you own or manage a business, I would highly recommend embracing this idea that everyone is a potential customer by the nature of our connection to all people. A welcoming culture toward all goes much further, in my opinion, than one of exclusivity and narrow targeting. I realize this runs counter to traditional business philosophy, and I'm not advocating that companies avoid trying to better understand who their customers are. But I am suggesting that marketing campaigns not be designed to exclude anyone. Targeting customers is wise. Excluding people you assume would never be your customers is not.

This is a powerful realization because it means that you can cast a wider net than you may have thought possible when selling your products or services if you first prioritize finding the connection point with people. It means that half the battle of winning customers is already won. You don't have to create a connection; you just have peel back the layers to find the connection that's already there. It means that, potentially, everyone can be your customer or add to your business by virtue of this fact.

On an individual basis, embracing this notion of connection is extremely relevant. It means that our stories and experiences matter to other people. How many of us have been convinced that our experiences and our view of the world don't amount to a hill of beans? How many people refuse to believe that they alone can create a ripple that changes the world, that we all have something important to contribute, and that we can communicate something meaningful to others from our unique vantage point?

Just as the people sitting behind the end zone at a football game have a different perspective on the action than someone sitting at center field, no one else can see the world exactly as you can. It means that you can enjoy being an individual and a member of a collective at the same time. That we're all at the same football game called "life" makes our story relatable. *Our vantage point* makes our story unique and worth hearing.

To the ones who say, "I don't have what it takes to stand out and make a difference," I encourage you to get creative to cut through the noise. Share your story authentically, as only you can, and watch what happens next. To those people who feel unimportant, as though they have nothing special to offer, I say that your story does matter and that there is no one better qualified to share your perspective than *you.*

So not only is it possible that other people want to hear your story, in a sense you have a *responsibility* to stand up and be heard. When you share your relatable perspective on a story, you do others a service because it gives them fresh perspective and an opportunity to reflect on their own experience. Many of the thousands of e-mails I've received begin with congratulations for the success of the video but quickly lead into people sharing their own customer-service nightmares. Others have written to explain how they and their friends exchanged stories for hours following a viewing of "UBG." So, not only does it feel good to be creative and share your experience, it's almost wrong not to.

I BELIEVE SIMPLY WATCHING THE VIDEO and the sharing of stories that followed is akin to opening a pressure valve that releases pent-up anger and frustration in others. For me, the greatest accomplishment of "UBG" is that what my friends and I created reminds people of individual experiences that bind us to one another, showing that we are connected. For four minutes, my video stole that amount of time away from the superficial distractions that try to convince us otherwise. That has been most gratifying to me.

Here's an example. Among the many e-mails I've received about the videos, some stand out more than others. I recall a story someone shared about a trip through JFK airport in New York. The person was being shuttled from one terminal to another along with other travelers when, for some reason, someone began singing the last part of the "United Breaks Guitars" chorus. Apparently several strangers joined in to sing the last line of the song, and everyone on the shuttle laughed out loud. A minute later, they arrived at the terminal and disbanded, likely never to see each other again. The writer of the story called it the greatest example of the *power of one* he'd ever seen. In a way, I think he was right.

While I suspect he was referring to my individual accomplishment with the video, I think it is more correct to say that "UBG" offers a concrete example of our collective power and connectedness, even if we are unaware it exists. What I love about the story isn't that a lot of people knew my song. What I love is that, for a moment, complete strangers came together to share in something that made their day better, and that something I had written had facilitated that. It reminded me, once again, that I didn't accomplish anything on my own. It was the millions of people who took the time to watch the video who made it news. It was the average person—telling friends, authors, bloggers, and the media that spread the story—who deepened the impact of the trilogy. The *one* in this case comprised the *many,* and there is undoubtedly power in that.

It's now clear to me, having had a lot of time to consider "UBG," that the deep ripples it caused were initiated by the fact that I stood up and creatively shared a unique story honestly and fairly, but also that it required my connection with everyone else for it to spread. Yes, social media facilitated it, but it first took an individual and the existence of a connection to a mass audience to succeed. It also required a universally accepted message founded upon nonconfrontation to spread so quickly.

If you throw a pebble into a calm pond, the ripples travel effortlessly to all banks because the water creating the splash is seamlessly connected to the rest of the water in the pond. However, if the ripples are impeded anywhere along their travels, they stop. To me, the same analogy proves our connection to one another. The video, and news of it, traveled quickly around the world because it resonated with everyone. The message was calm, true, and direct . . . and it was able to resonate because it communicated at the level of universal truth, where ripples run unimpeded.

I see that we are connected with others more clearly than ever since July 2009. While some people might choose the perspective that "United Breaks Guitars" was one man's angry tirade against a vulnerable corporation, my experience and careful consideration says that it goes a lot deeper than that. We are connected; and, for me, knowing that fact changes everything.

♫ ♪ ♫ ♪ ♫

Part IV

CAREER IMPACTS FOLLOWING THE FRENZY

Chapter 14

MUSIC SALES JUMP AND SONGWRITING SOARS

The day after launching "United Breaks Guitars," everything changed for me. It happened that fast. With all the attention the video was receiving, the things you'd expect to occur did, and the first major impact on my career was a sharp increase in music sales. People started paying attention to this Dave Carroll guy, and although we wouldn't be able to offer the "UBG" single on iTunes for three weeks, my *Perfect Blue* recording was available there, and **DaveCarrollMusic.com** offered the "UBG" single and all of my recordings as digital downloads. And finally, if you wanted the physical CD *Perfect Blue,* you could also order it through my website.

Our mom has been a constant source of help for Don and me and has been the backbone of Sons of Maxwell and my solo career when it comes to mail orders and bookkeeping. She's been doing that for as long as I can remember, and in the early days before e-commerce, with every mail-order CD, she was so happy that anyone was supporting her sons' careers that she would knit them a dishcloth as padding for the envelope. People loved that touch, but those days were long gone when the orders started pouring in on July 8, 2009.

My parents live only one street away from me in Waverley, and when I called to ask how sales were affected by the video, Mom suggested that I drop by to see her and check it out firsthand. When I got there, I called out to her to see where she was. She called back from the basement and said I should look in the living room.

When I stuck my head around the corner, I saw that the entire living-room sofa was covered in yellow manila envelopes, packed and labeled with CDs ready to mail. They were piled ten high, in two rows, for the whole length of the sofa. I called back downstairs, "This is incredible!"

She replied, "That's our third sofa full!"

I laughed and yelled back downstairs that we needed to expand the business. "Get in the car, Mom. We're going to buy you a sectional . . . and retire the knitting needles . . . you're getting a loom!"

I also began to find that feedback from people who were buying the music was overwhelmingly positive, and I was quickly building my music fan base. I'd receive comments like, "I'm sorry this had to happen to you in order for me to discover your other music, but I love it." One song in particular, called "Now," stands out as the one that seems to elicit the strongest reaction in new listeners.

That song is on my *Perfect Blue* CD and was inspired by the work of authors Wayne Dyer and Eckhart Tolle. The idea centers on living in the present moment, and after reading Tolle's *The Power of Now,* I decided to try to capture the essence of the message in a song.

"Now" has become a favorite song of mine to sing, and it has a big impact on audiences. In fact, Tolle's publisher, Constance Kellough, phoned me after hearing it to say they felt my song was the soundtrack to Eckhart's message and "the audio portal into stillness." Tolle's message has been embraced by millions of people around the world, and many fans have happened upon this song after the "UBG" videos had piqued their curiosity about my other music. I've received heartwarming stories about how "Now" has brought peace and serenity to those going through the toughest of times, and I believe that other people are meant to hear it. For that reason, in the "Lyrics" section at the back of this book I've included the words to "Now" and a free link to the recording as a gift. I welcome you to enjoy it.

One morning I received a powerful message from a woman explaining that her mother had just passed away in palliative care only hours earlier. Her mother had been confined to bed in her last days and often enjoyed watching "United Breaks Guitars" to lighten her mood. When she wanted to hear some of my other music, she asked her daughter to order the *Perfect Blue* CD, and she discovered "Now."

She said her mom would play it often because it helped give her an amazing sense of calm, and just before she died, she asked her daughter to play the song again. While it played, she passed away peacefully. I can tell you that as a songwriter, I can think of no greater honor than to write something so meaningful to another that it helps that individual cope with life's greatest challenges. While that song was a gift to her mother, in this case my own music was a gift to me—realizing this may be one of the most meaningful impacts of "United Breaks Guitars" on my career.

Another unexpected result of "UBG" was an increase in offers to play gigs that wouldn't have occurred otherwise. In October of 2011, the band and I traveled to Siberia, Saint Petersburg, and Moscow for our first tour of Russia, and "United Breaks Guitars" is the reason I was asked to travel there. The trip was a great success, and just about everyone at the shows had seen the video. Despite the fact that most audience members could not speak English, "UBG" proved to be a great icebreaker to connect new fans to my other music.

The video has also been helpful with English-speaking audiences who may not have known my name. As an example, in March 2009 I was invited to Ireland to join Canadian songwriters Dave Gunning, Christina Martin, and Terry Penny for my first tour of the homeland. The shows involved each of us taking a turn introducing a song and playing it in what has become known as a songwriters' circle. Each night, when it came my turn and I began relating the "UBG" experience, you could hear a murmur of Irish voices as listeners realized I was behind a story they knew very well. I relish how the Irish have a love of language and the ability to make even swearwords sound poetic as I'd listen to them whisper things like "Dat's the f--king guy who wrote dat song."

Back in July, prior to that Ireland trip, a senior agent from one of North America's leading music agencies flew to Halifax, and we agreed that he should represent me. For a short time, I thought the bookings from his agency would start pouring in. From my perspective, I was hoping that he would work his contacts to get me placed on higher-profile stages and playing to bigger audiences. I think he hoped that his phone would ring off the hook from people wanting to throw money at me. There are several agencies that represent so many bands that I wonder if their business model is simply to put themselves between as many artists and people looking to hire them as possible, when serving the artists' best interests would involve a proactive effort to find meaningful gigs.

Either way, my experience with this agency was a real disappointment. After several months, my agent failed to bring a single gig to the table. Worldwide media attention, millions of YouTube hits, a 20-year career, with ten CDs . . . and not a single performance contract from him. Once again, I was reminded that DIY (do it yourself) is your best option if the people working for you either don't believe in you, can't appreciate your value, or aren't prepared to do a little work for their pay. That agency may do good work for other artists, but they no longer represent me.

WHILE ALL THIS WAS GOING ON, the rest of my team and I were working like crazy and stayed very busy. It was in late July 2009 when I got a call from Paul Sparkes, an executive from CTV in Toronto asking if we could meet in Halifax that week. (CTV is Canada's largest private television broadcaster.) I didn't know Paul but welcomed the meeting, and a few days later, he explained during lunch that Canadian broadcasters were in a dispute with the country's cable-TV providers over the fact that cable companies were not obliged to pay a fee for local news and other programming.

The marketplace had changed in recent years, and revenues had fallen because ad dollars were now diluted across so many new sources, such as the Internet. Paul explained that without revenue sharing from cable, broadcasters would have to sell television stations, and that local programming would fade as the broadcasts became more centralized. The national regulatory body on such things, the CRTC (Canadian Radio-television Telecommunications Commission), would be deciding the outcome of this dispute. Paul asked if I believed in the cause, and could CTV commission me to write a song and produce a video with the goal of acquiring grassroots support for local programming?

On the surface it may appear ironic that the old-school media was reaching out for support from a YouTube innovator like me, but Paul Sparkes understood that embracing what works is how companies stay relevant today. CTV was looking for public support and awareness of the issues, and knowing that the people he wanted to reach were congregating online, he contacted me because of my familiarity to Canadians at the time and my ability to communicate a message. In this case, CTV did exactly what all companies should be doing: embrace new ideas that have proven successful in order to stay competitive and relevant in their customers' eyes.

Personally, I said yes to CTV for a few reasons. I asked myself, *What would happen if local news coverage evaporated from the Canadian landscape?* In our travels across the country, Don and I had often enjoyed the support of community and regional broadcasters promoting our shows. Countless other independent artists do as well. We've performed on many of the local breakfast shows on TV and had our events publicized on local newscasts.

I am also a supporter of the annual IWK Health Centre telethon aired by the regional CTV affiliate in Halifax each year. My son, Flynn, was born at this local children's hospital and received amazing care, so I began wondering if there could be a telethon without a local TV station. What if one day Flynn needed help from the IWK and his care were less than it could have been because of millions in lost fund-raising? If local stations would close without fees from cable, I believed those closures would not only be bad for the country and my community, but potentially for my family. I agreed to take on the project and started doing my research.

As though I didn't have enough going on as it was, before "UBG" was released I had been diagnosed with three minor hernias and had scheduled a trip to Toronto in August to a clinic that works exclusively on hernial procedures. The technique at the Shouldice Hospital is highly effective, and even though getting this done wasn't an emergency, the ruptures also weren't going to get better on their own, so I decided to get it over with as planned and arrived in Toronto for repairs.

I'd be there for a week, and between two surgeries and some recovery time, the plan was to get as much work done as possible. At Shouldice, they use local anesthetic, so although you're dopey during the operation, you're definitely awake. During the surgery I recall joking with the doctor, who was a fan of "UBG," that I'd make him famous if he cut anything more than he was supposed to. I also recall a nurse coming over to meet me, and we talked a bit about the video while I was on the table.

I made some good headway in my downtime that week, though. The hospital had a common area with a piano and, as luck would have it, a guitar. Each day I would shuffle my way to the common area and settle into a position that didn't hurt in order to play a while. Eventually I just started bringing the guitar to my room and ended up completing two songs at Shouldice. The first one was the CTV song that would later became "The Cable Song." The second was inspired by a challenge from the president of a company called Intrado, a story I will go into in the next chapter. It would appear that for me, nothing gets the creative juices flowing like some good old-fashioned surgery. When I returned home, I promptly called Ferguson Music Productions to arrange to record both new songs within the next few days.

When the song for CTV was ready that next week, I called Paul Sparkes asking if I could present it to the CTV stakeholders in person. They booked me on a return flight to Toronto the next day, and my father-in-law, Brent, and I were welcomed at the head office at 299 Queen Street West. There we sat in the executive boardroom of the famous MuchMusic Building as I played the recording for Paul, along with Ivan Fecan and Susanne Boyce, two of the most influential people in Canadian broadcasting, whom Paul later described as "the Mr. and Mrs. Television of Canada." They listened to the song once and loved it. That was it. I was hired, and they left Paul, Brent, and me to work out the particulars of the video and the deadlines.

Within weeks of that meeting, we had reassembled the "UBG" team and shot the video for "The Cable Song." We had a great time poking fun at cable executives, placing them in a goofy-looking cow costume, mingling among real cows in a failed attempt to make off with a farmer's milk for free. CTV played the full-length video countless times during regular programming across their many stations, exposure that music videos rarely enjoy otherwise. The dispute between broadcasters and the cable providers went all the way to the Supreme Court of Canada. In the end, the broadcasters won, and I was told that my video contributed to a very tight decision and was influencing public policy and the law!

So as you can see, another significant impact of "United Breaks Guitars" on my career has become the commissioning of songs for others. I truly enjoy the process.

I recently finished writing a song for Sandvik Coromant, the world's leader in cutting tools. Prior to January 2011, the most attention I had paid to cutting tools involved reaching for the scissors, but after speaking at their event in Orlando and meeting their sales and marketing team, I got excited about cutting tools because *they* were excited about them. It was infectious, and I suggested to the president that he let me capture the essence of their message in a song to inspire their audience. He agreed. I loved learning about the industry and enjoy being inspired by passionate people.

Sandvik Coromant loves their song, and although this tune will never be played on the radio, it has real meaning to the people for whom it was intended. I'm getting to learn about worlds I'd never otherwise have been exposed to and am having a positive impact on companies that care about customers. I certainly didn't see that in my future before "UBG."

♬ ♪ ♬ ♪ ♬

Chapter 15

"EVERYDAY HEROES" IS BORN

I made another incredible connection when I got an e-mail from a man named George Heinrichs in July 2009. George introduced himself as the president of a U.S. company called Intrado, and a fan of UBG, and he asked if the band could come to Longmont, Colorado, to play an event planned for October of that year. He had appreciated how UBG was presented in "the Canadian way" (nonconfrontationally and with humor). I jumped at the chance, having never been to Colorado. We spoke on the phone shortly after, and George asked if I'd be interested in coming to their headquarters even sooner to meet and learn firsthand what Intrado does as a company. I was intrigued and, again, was happy to say yes.

It turns out that Intrado is a major service provider for the 911 system and is involved in almost every emergency call in the United States. A thousand people work in Longmont at their high-security complex, and George took me on an impressive tour of his facility. Near the end, we stopped at what I liken to an interpretive center, where you can walk to various stations and read about and listen to some carefully chosen past 911 calls. Some of them are very moving and end tragically, and I suppose the purpose of having this area in the building is to remind people why Intrado exists and the value their work provides.

It was at that time that George mentioned he knew that I was a volunteer firefighter and that Don had become a full-time firefighter. He asked if I'd ever written a song for first responders, and I explained that I'd considered it but hadn't done so yet. He challenged me to give it a try sometime, and we continued on with the tour. I stayed in Longmont a couple of days, was duly impressed with the company, and looked forward to returning in October to perform with the band.

As mentioned earlier, it was in the Shouldice Hospital that I wrote "The Cable Song" for CTV, as well as what would become "Everyday Heroes." The approach I took for the latter was to adopt the perspective of the relationship between first responders and those in need. Intrado is making use of incredible technology to help the 911 system work, but the entire system ultimately depends on the integrity of the people who answer those calls. It's actually quite amazing that when a person needs help and dials 911, there are strangers willing to rush to his or her aid because they promised that they would. The whole thing rests on a promise. That idea is the foundation of the song "Everyday Heroes." A week after returning home from Toronto, I recorded and sent the song off to George for his feedback.

I'd say his response was good. He said, "When you come here to play in October, make a compilation CD that includes 'Everyday Heroes' and I'll buy 1,000 copies." That was cool! It's also worth pointing out that by having been independent throughout my music career, I still owned all my own music publishing rights to everything I'd recorded. That meant I was free to make compilation-CD deals like the one for George quickly and give the customer a unique product that a signed artist could not.

THE RETURN TRIP TO PLAY THE INTRADO event in October turned into something much bigger. We performed a full set of music that day in a huge tent in the company parking lot with seats for 1,000 employees. There was a large stage bookended by two huge projection screens, and as we performed "Everyday Heroes" for the first time, George had arranged to show a series of still images from real 911 scenes. The song, those images, and the fact that the audience was filled with people who are passionate about the service they provide resulted in a long and moving standing ovation.

After the show, George took me aside to say that he was moved by the reaction and that he felt other people should experience "Everyday Heroes" as well. Then he made a generous offer, saying, "If you're interested in making a video for this song, Intrado would be happy to pay for it."

Talk about things that never happen in the music business! Someone believed enough in my story and my song that they wanted to donate significant money to help share it with others. Intrado is welcome to use the video as they please, but George gave the funding freely and wanted no ownership of the song. Best of all, he allowed all the creative control to remain in our hands. Trust me—in the music business, that gets filed in the "just doesn't happen" folder.

So in May 2010, I hired Curve Productions to coordinate a two-day video shoot for "Everyday Heroes," and for a change, I had a respectable budget for crew and lights and actors. Halifax Regional Fire & Emergency cooperated by donating fire trucks and allowing real firefighters to participate. In fact, my brother, Don, plays the leading firefighter role.

As for engaging the help of the police with the video, that was another story. I suppose most of the time it's a good thing to have a clean criminal record, but in this case, it meant that they didn't know me when I approached them. The Halifax police, it turns out, were more cautious about getting involved in this video project, and they respectfully declined. We had no choice but to get creative. There's a popular Canadian TV show called *Trailer Park Boys,* and we paid to use the police cars, uniforms, and other props from that show for the law-enforcement components in our video.

Even with the funding from Intrado, we still needed to cut corners wherever possible, so I dropped by my parents' house and said, "Hey, Mom, we're shooting the video for 'Everyday Heroes.' Do you mind if we take a day to use your house for a domestic-violence scene?"

She asked, "Okay, when?"

I replied, "Mother's Day!"

She scowled, before reluctantly saying, "Okay." I wasn't done, though. Then I asked if she could cater it as well.

She nearly choked but got out the words: "How many people?" I told her we'd have to feed about 40, and she looked at me as though I had two heads—and as though having two heads was a bad thing.

After a minute, Mom conceded with an expression that suggested that if I had an additional request, it should wait for another day. I thanked her and left, but on my way out the door, my dad was quick to put in his own two cents. "What do we need all these actors for? Let's just shoot a reality show." The door closed as I listened to him laughing at his own joke.

We completed the video and posted it on YouTube, where it continues to move people today. We went a step further and created a website for "Everyday Heroes" called **911Song.com**. The purpose of the site is not only to show the video, but to give people an opportunity to share their gratitude for first responders. There are many police officers, firefighters, paramedics, and dispatch workers who deserve to be acknowledged for going the extra mile for strangers, and **911Song.com** is designed to collect those thoughts and become a destination for gratitude.

Once again, "United Breaks Guitars" had led to something completely unforeseen, and I've tried to pay it forward in the same spirit that George funded that video. I'm including the lyrics to "Everyday Heroes" for you to enjoy with this book (along with a free download link), and I hope you will take a minute and visit the website to view the video and share a grateful message of your own.

♬ ♪ ♬ ♪ ♬

Chapter 16

BECOMING A KEYNOTE SPEAKER, AUTHOR, AND ADVOCATE

It has been an exciting change to take the stage and use my storytelling skills in a completely different way. In addition to musical performances, today I am a busy keynote speaker in the areas of customer service, branding, social media, and self-empowerment as I travel the world sharing my story and some of the lessons I've learned. Because it's so relatable and broadly sweeping, I've found that this experience is a fit for almost any event, and I have received enthusiastic responses from diverse audiences across Canada, the U.S., the U.K., the Czech Republic, Australia, and Russia.

The speaking-engagement side of things started in September 2009, when Montana-based RightNow Technologies (the company that would ultimately sponsor my trip to South by Southwest) called and asked for my availability to share my story at their Colorado Springs event in October 2009. The woman told me that 700 of the world's biggest brands would be there.

I said, "Yes, I'd love to do it."

The woman continued, "I assume you're hired to speak about 'United Breaks Guitars' all the time these days?"

By answering "Yes," I may have been overstating my experience slightly because in reality, I'd never done any public speaking about "UBG" . . . or anything else. Even in our many concerts, Don had always done most of the talking. I had given all kinds of media interviews, where I would speak for about 90 seconds, but the thought of a 40-minute keynote address to an audience sitting right in front of me . . . that was a whole other kettle of fish.

Back in my university days, I'd started my own summer business doing odd jobs and said yes to every inquiry, whether I had experience doing what was asked or not. There *was* that one exception when I was asked to rewire someone's house (which I actually considered until my dad, an electrician, begged me not to try it). However, I've discovered that saying yes to opportunity usually works out if you try hard enough, and because old habits are hard to break, my answer to RightNow Technologies just kind of spilled out. So before I knew it, I was booked to speak in Colorado Springs.

As the date got closer, the RightNow conference planners were eager to get an advance copy of my PowerPoint presentation, so I called my father-in-law and asked, "What exactly *is* a PowerPoint presentation, anyway?" I knew it was some kind of tool for speeches but had never used it. Musicians don't require PowerPoint as a rule, but I was going to need it now, so I assembled the content and Brent went about creating a slideshow for me while I bought some time with RightNow Technologies, saying we were "tweaking" the presentation for their event.

In the intervening weeks, and while recovering from my hernia surgery, we produced "The Cable Song" video—and I continued doing interviews, worked on "UBG2," went to Washington, played shows, and also scrambled to organize a U.S. immigration visa to perform stateside. Essentially I did my best to match the pace of activity. Before I knew it, the trip to deliver my first keynote had arrived.

When I got to Colorado Springs, I discovered that the Broadmoor hotel, where I was booked, is a AAA Five Diamond resort. Unlike a Motel 6, they don't just leave a light on for you; the Broadmoor leaves *all* the lights on for you, and I was blown away by what a fantastic hotel it was.

I went to the convention room the night before for a rehearsal, and it was huge. The tables for 700 were set, the stage that I'd speak on seemed immense, and there were enormous screens on either side of it. My presentation would be videotaped and shown on the two 20-foot screens while I attempted to give my first-ever speech. I was a little intimidated.

Brent had just created the PowerPoint show in New Brunswick, so this rehearsal was the first time I had seen the layout of the presentation. I remember the look on the conference planners' faces as they realized I needed instructions on how to work the slide-advancing remote (which had two arrows only: forward and backward).

To my credit, it was a short tutorial, but what alarmed them more was that, rather than casually glancing at the video monitors for cues, I was practically bending at the waist to read them. My eyes were devouring those PowerPoint slides! The conference planners were too professional to panic, but I wouldn't have held it against them if they would have run from the room screaming as though their hair was on fire.

I gladly accepted some tips on how to move around the stage and promised them that I was just getting settled, and that by the morning, the real thing would be different. I went back to my room and worked on my presentation until I had it right. As a musician, I've always found that the real performance is better than practice, so I was banking on that experience to give me confidence come showtime, as it always had before. I simply reminded myself that I was there to tell my story and was the only one qualified to do so, and like the lyrics in "UBG," I'd simply tell it like it happened.

In the end, the presentation was a big hit, and I felt completely comfortable onstage. Since then, my presentation skills have greatly improved, but for a first time, I couldn't have been happier with the result. The audience enjoyed the story, and RightNow was pleased as well.

What helped break the ice that day was another mishap with United Airlines. I had arrived in Colorado from Regina, Saskatchewan, and the only direct flight to Denver was with United. I decided to take my chances but carried my guitar on board. When I got to Denver, my guitar and I were ready to go, but my luggage didn't make it, and they couldn't say for sure where it was! So on the day of my initiation to public speaking, my lost luggage became front-page news in *The New York Times* business section and the opening comment of my presentation. The audience loved it, and another wave of media attention began with CNN and others.

I HAVE SINCE TRAVELED much more confidently to speaking engagements all over the world, but one of the highlights for me as a speaker came in January 2010 when I was invited to share the stage with Gene Simmons of the rock band KISS. If you would have told me in 2008 that I'd be opening for Gene Simmons, I would have questioned the musical fit, but I still would have gone along with it. If you would have told me that it wasn't going to be for music, but rather at a speaking event on branding, I might have had you fitted for a straitjacket. That's exactly what happened, though, and I found myself delivering my presentation on branding to Gene Simmons and hundreds of other people at the Atlantic Brand Confabulation in Moncton, New Brunswick. That was a great experience.

Gene is a branding expert and a very intelligent man, so I enjoyed his presentation and learned a lot. He's a big believer in trademarking everything, and when he noticed that my company logo (the broken-guitar chalk outline from "UBG") had no ™ beside it, he jokingly warned me to trademark it by the start of the next week or he'd steal it! At least I hoped he was joking. Just in case, I called a lawyer that Monday morning.

Gene advocates protecting yourself legally and then being litigious with copyright infringement. While suing people isn't necessarily my thing, I'm also not worth $500 million. We met the next day, and he had some helpful tips on some things I should do to protect myself—tips that later proved very valuable.

Becoming an author was never even on the horizon when I released "UBG." However, I've come to enjoy the process of writing and getting published. I love communicating and reaching people with a meaningful message. I've experienced doing it with a song, and I've enjoyed doing it with music videos as well. Since "UBG," I've discovered that public speaking offers a unique opportunity to connect with people, and now I'm even more grateful to be enjoying the experience of using the written word to convey my message, too. In fact, it feels quite natural, since the methods of a songwriter, speaker, author, and advocate are simply different ways of telling a story, and I enjoy the challenge of working within the confines of each medium to achieve that.

As I mentioned, I am a big admirer of author Wayne Dyer, and I sent him a copy of my song "Now" through his daughter Tracy, who was a fan of "UBG." I'd wanted to give the song to Wayne as a thank-you for helping inspire it.

Tracy told me that she had shown her dad "UBG" and that he loved it. He thought that I should write a book about my experience and how I handled a frustrating situation nonconfrontationally. She added that I ought to take him up on his advice and that she thought maybe he could help me get a book deal with his publisher, Hay House. I couldn't believe it.

I've still never met Wayne Dyer or spoken to him directly, but Hay House's president and CEO, Reid Tracy, accepted my request to talk about a book. After speaking on the phone, he agreed to publish my story if I could write an acceptable sample chapter and a book outline.

While some people would assume that hiring a ghostwriter would be the only option for an inexperienced author, I decided to go for it myself. There was that old habit again of jumping in, with or without credentials, to gain and enjoy a new experience. After all, who is better qualified to tell my story? And if I simply let someone else tell it, when in my life would anyone ask me to write a book again? This was the time to try it, and I'm glad that I did.

Thankfully Reid enjoyed what I sent, because I was offered a conditional book deal on my first contact with a publisher. I'm told that just doesn't happen, and to say I'm lucky would be a gross understatement.

THE OTHER SIDE OF THIS WHOLE ADVENTURE involved breaking new ground as a consumer advocate. Early in the "UBG" project, I saw the video's impact as a conversation starter for everyone else's customer-service nightmares. In those early days, I was swamped with e-mails of support and frequent requests to help others who felt frustrated and hopeless. "UBG" had become a kind of bad-customer-service meeting ground.

My father-in-law always saw a wider potential for "UBG" than most. Brent's experience as a telecommunications executive, and having negotiated a large online learning contract with Nortel (a multinational telecom-equipment manufacturer) gave him a broader understanding about building an online business from scratch and making it scalable.

Since I've always been a big believer in good customer service, with the influx of e-mail from people as frustrated in this arena as I was, Brent suggested that we create a website called Right Side of Right. The idea was that this site would be a meeting place for people to share bad customer-service experiences, with the goal of getting them resolved. Maybe companies would become aware of negative stories on my site and reach out to customers to resolve conflicts before they got out of hand. That was the concept, at least.

It was an excellent idea, and we created the website to do that, but in reality no one on my team had the resources or the time to bring it to its full potential. With this endeavor, we'd certainly reached our limits as to what we could handle on our own. So I continued to help people whenever possible and accepted that maybe this role would be more of a hobby than a larger enterprise or entity.

Recently, though, I was introduced to a fellow Canadian named Richard Hue whose own customer-service nightmare inspired him to create change. Rather than make a music video, Richard used his strengths to develop an online customer-service resolution platform called **Gripevine.com**. He and his web-designing co-founder Chris Caple knew my story, and when they saw my Right Side of Right website, they could see that we shared the same view about conflict resolution. As a result, I have welcomed the invitation to join them as a co-founder of what I believe will become the leading destination for resolving customer complaints in the coming years.

Gripevine.com is a fully realized version of Right Side of Right. It is a user-friendly "gripe center" that invites customers to share the issue they have with, say, Company X. It is not a place to simply bash brands and complain, however. Gripevine was created to resolve problems and improve the world by doing so. The intent is to take the pain out of complaining for the customers, and the pain out of complaints for companies.

When someone plants a gripe on Gripevine, the website's powerful back-end software tools take that gripe and send it to the right people at Company X to resolve. The degree to which it gets resolved to the customer's satisfaction results in a letter grade determined by customers, and that letter grade rests in plain view for all to see on that company's Gripevine page.

The intention is for businesses to be made aware of problems more directly, shaving minutes off resolving each complaint. All of those minutes could add up to millions of dollars in savings for companies. By delivering better customer service, they can control their Gripevine evaluation grade and use it as a source of pride to attract new customers and promote themselves externally.

Gripevine is a win-win solution platform that understands the relationship between consumers and companies, and it strives to bring the two together. Customers don't really complain without a reason, and no respectable company sets out to deliver bad products or services. Gripevine facilitates conflict resolution, and companies that understand social media realize that their customers will be talking about them whether they embrace Gripevine or not. Joining the conversation is the only logical alternative, and Gripevine is the answer to managing this new opportunity.

I am thrilled to be a founding partner in Gripevine and am now active in communicating the merits of all it can become. I believe that every minute people spend frustrated and angry in a customer-service maze is a minute they aren't doing something worthwhile . . . so "United Breaks Guitars" has led me here, to a new opportunity to satisfy my mission statement of improving the world, one experience at a time.

My goal with everything I'm doing—whether it is as a performer, songwriter, speaker, writer, or consumer advocate—is to eliminate as many negative ripples traveling the world as I can. Replacing negative ripples with positive ones creates the potential for lasting change and the possibility of leaving the world a better place than how we found it.

♬ ♪ ♬ ♪ ♬

Chapter 17

TAKING MY MUSIC AND MESSAGE TO THE WORLD

You know you've made a pretty big splash with something when you hear *Jeopardy!* host Alex Trebek say your name not as a contestant, but as he's reading the board itself! He said, "For $1,000, under 'Breaking News,' the answer is: *Nearly 10 million YouTubers saw Dave Carroll's clip, called this 'Friendly Skies' airline 'Breaks Guitars.'*" On that special episode, it was the computer player, Watson, that beat the two former champion contestants to the buzzer and replied: "What is United?"

It was February 2011 when that show aired, and while I was at a hockey game with my dad, my Facebook and Twitter feeds started lighting up with the news.

So much has happened that I've enjoyed telling you about, but once I got into the writing of this book, I was unsure how to end it. My life continues to expand in all directions, and my video continues to impact people in the strangest of places. Without question, social media has afforded every single person with access to a computer the ability to share a message with a mass audience. My video has inspired others to take action, or at least believe that they have the power to be heard.

"UBG" has compelled huge companies to reevaluate how they handle customer-service complaints and to rethink the concept of branding in the age of social media. To illustrate this, it is interesting to look at the Canadian company called Radian 6, which sells social-media monitoring tools to companies around the world.

The tools Radian 6 provides collect comments and messages made by people using any kind of social media to refer to a specific brand online. This allows companies to be more aware of what people are saying about them and, conceivably, allows them to respond quickly to a "UBG"-style social-media wildfire before it becomes uncontrollable. Solutions like the ones Radian 6 provides are in huge demand today, and I have been told that the company has made reference to my video on numerous occasions as one example when promoting the need for their tools. This demand is further evidenced by the fact that they were recently bought out for nearly $350 million after only a few years in business. In this way, "United Breaks Guitars" has certainly changed my life and the lives of others to varying degrees.

Life, however, is a journey and not a destination, so as my story continues to evolve and lead to new and unexpected things, I look forward to embracing these opportunities and evaluating them from the perspective of where I am now and where they may take me. As far as the book is concerned, though, I think I have found an appropriate place to land.

Everyone's lives, my own included, are products of the endless series of choices we make. It's as though we're continually being presented with two doors and having to decide which one to walk through. Many people have felt that "UBG" was blind luck; that the incident came upon a musician at a time when social media was in its infancy, during a slow news period, and when customers around the world were like fuel waiting for a spark. Others give me too much credit and suggest that everything I did was part of a carefully calculated plan. I'd say the truth lies somewhere in the middle.

I've discovered that sometimes the best choices presented to me have been wide-open doorways that are easy to walk through. Other times I've found that the easiest path is the one to avoid. I've had to squeeze through the cracks of some doors, and as I learned as a firefighter, when you're on the wrong side of a locked door, the answer may be to smash it to smithereens.

When it comes to choosing which doors to open, we're influenced by the people who surround us. I'm most grateful for having had such positive support in my life to help guide me on my path. Whether they were lessons learned from my dad at a bedtime sing-along or advice from a roundtable "meeting of the minds" in the first week of "UBG," I am fortunate to have been surrounded by people who have wanted the best for me.

Some of my greatest teachers have been authors, like Wayne Dyer, who have contributed a single idea that gave me pause to consider a better perspective on life. Often one idea can influence small decisions that result in the biggest changes, and at times my greatest role models have been people I try to emulate because the way in which they lead their own lives *is* the idea.

As this book began to take shape, it occurred to me that there is one element that determines not only my success, but everyone's. There is one emotion that can fuel our dreams, and if it's absent, we will find them unfulfilled. The degree to which it is present determines when we take action and the times we choose not to. This magical element is *caring*.

Caring is fundamental to all life and akin to oxygen that breathes life into all of us. Without it, why would you take the time to develop goals, and in its absence, what reason or purpose would drive you through life's obstacles? Likewise, caring is the silent partner to passion. How can you be energized about something you don't care about, and what kind of quality can you expect in anything you do if the process you went through to create it is devoid of care?

EVERYTHING ABOUT "UBG" was founded upon caring. I spent time in the United customer-service maze because I cared about my guitar and wanted the company responsible for the damage to care about it, too. I wrote the songs and produced the videos because I didn't want to have to experience that frustration again and because I wanted to help others avoid a similar fate. I found myself surrounded by thousands of people who e-mailed me to say that they cared about my story and supported me, including United employees, whom I later found myself caring about in return.

I wrote the songs to the best of my ability in order to make them as enjoyable as possible because I care about the minutes I'm asking people to invest in listening to me. I invited musicians who take pride in their playing to perform on the tracks because they care about the music they produce. Scott Ferguson made many small adjustments to the audio mixes of the trilogy because he loves his part in creating great-sounding songs.

Everyone at Curve Productions realizes that anyone who views the videos is seeing their work, also, and I can tell you they care about that. Everyone involved was asked to contribute what they love doing. As a result, "United Breaks Guitars" reflects the nature of the ingredients that went into making it. The fact that so much care was injected into every aspect of this project is one very important element that made "UBG" so entertaining and successful.

I wish that all products and all content in this world were developed with the same level of care. What a difference that would make!

Two sayings come to mind when I think about *content:*

1. *Garbage in = garbage out.* If you want to produce quality, you need quality ingredients, and that requires care!
2. *Content is king.* This is an old one but has never been truer than in the age of social media.

There are sites all over the Internet screaming for quality content, because unfortunately, not everyone who contributes online material cares about their product. It's a fact that the best thing you can do to stand out in a noisy online environment is to be committed to how your product looks and sounds. I've proved that you don't need a big budget to cut through the noise, and YouTube has plenty of videos with more hits than "UBG," but ones that leave a lasting an impression are relatively rare. If you care that people may choose to spend some of their valuable time looking at you, your content will likely raise itself up and stand above the "clutter." I have learned that the simple act of caring changes the outcome, and I challenge everyone to try it for themselves. It works.

The beauty of caring is that it's contagious and unlimited. Whereas anger is draining and self-defeating, caring is empowering and energizing. That's why I reject the notion that "UBG" was about a confrontation, and it's also why I don't see myself as a vigilante. Engaging in the creative aspect of the project lightened my load, and none of the effort ever felt like work.

Believe it or not, I want the best for United Airlines. I have gotten to know some of the employees, and I have a better understanding of how an airline operates—and it's a tricky business. More than ever, though, the one sure way to survive in a competitive industry is to inject caring into all aspects of your business.

If you care about the quality of what you produce, the employees who make it, the customers who support you, and how your products affect the world around you, then you become relevant to others. If your team members feel cared for and respected, they will care for and respect the customers whom they serve.

If your products are made with care, then customers will value your work and tell their friends. If what you make is good for the environment or improves the world in some way, people will care more about *you* as a company and as a person. Whether you run a multibillion-dollar airline or want to make a $150 viral video, the formula is the same . . . and it starts and ends with caring.

I have certainly found that when you care about others, you get it all back and more. The outpouring of support I received was incredibly uplifting. The knowledge that I have inspired others to get creative, as opposed to getting angry, is meaningful to me. Seeing my grandmother in the "UBG2" video brings a smile to all those who knew her and even those who didn't. People have hired me specifically because I handled the trilogy in a careful and nonconfrontational fashion. Yes, social media facilitated that and the fact that we are all connected made it possible, but caring is what energized an idea into action and then into reality.

I subscribe to the belief that all emotions hold a vibration and that love is the highest vibration there is. I see caring as the expression of that. I don't claim to be a spiritual guru or the poster child for living anger free, because I certainly have my days, but my intention is to create more space between the instances I spend in negative emotions such as anger and resentment. Maybe one day I'll be able to say that those are emotions I used to visit.

Having tried it both ways, I can say from experience that empowerment and lasting success are fueled by positive emotions and that caring is a fundamental aspect of the DNA in happiness. "United Breaks Guitars" has reminded me of that.

I've also come to realize the profound power of intention and that "like attracts like." My attitude from the time I vowed to release the trilogy has been positive, with unconditional gratitude and a belief that "UBG" was going to feel successful regardless of what happened. I've noticed that when I have been in a caring frame of mind, the right people or circumstances always appeared at precisely the right time to help me. This has happened so often in my life that I not only accept it, but I've now come to expect it. The opposite is also true, and in my most frustrating and trying times, my attitude and perspective has been a vibrational match to what I was receiving.

This all being said, where do I go from here? I think the answer is to welcome the new opportunities that I know are coming and embrace the ones that are in line with my mission statement. Whatever I choose to engage in, I've decided to approach it with a caring and positive attitude, and I know that when I do, I attract more of the same. In the process, I'll control the things within my reach and worry less about the things outside it. For whatever I can't do myself, I will partner with caring people who *can*. I believe I can achieve anything I set my mind to, and I'd like to share a few things I'm working on now and planning for the coming years, if for no other reason than simply because declaring your goals seems to help achieve them.

I've discovered how much I enjoy speaking to audiences, and I am actively developing this new aspect of my career. There are few speakers who involve live music in their presentations, and that makes me unique. Based on the positive reviews, this versatility seems to be very effective in reaching and engaging all kinds of audiences.

My life experiences add up to a message that is applicable to customer service, social media, branding, and self-empowerment, so there is potential to significantly grow the speaking part of my career and continue traveling the world as I share my messages and music.

I've taken on the role of consumer advocate since 2009, and I've always had an easier time sticking up for others than for myself. When I hear of people being mistreated, I want to help, especially when they *ask* for my help, so I believe that the customer-service platform I mentioned earlier, called Gripevine, may be the answer. It's in line with my message, it resolves conflict, and it is solutions based. I look forward to helping this platform reach its full potential.

Now that my son, Flynn, is two and half years old and loving music, I've been enjoying writing songs about him and his life. In fact, I recently completed a timely ditty called "We Pee in the Toilet" to help him potty train. It worked, and whenever he sits to pee, we celebrate with a "pee party." If he does anything more, we throw him a "bar shitsvah," but the song proves that music can be a good motivator and makes life fun for all ages. I expect it will not be long before I end up writing enough kids' songs for a full recording. I've also been approached to add music to some content included in a children's book series to reinforce its social messages in a fun way for school-age kids. This is another first but one that fits with my personal mission statement in a big way.

Less direct, maybe, but still interesting is the suggestion that I host a TV show having to do with customer service. While I turned down the offer from a popular newsmagazine to wear a hidden camera and travel through airports to expose faulty airline practices, I would entertain the idea of hosting a TV show if its purpose was to improve the world in some way. If part of the show involves a person taking off a shoe to hit someone, I'll leave that to Jerry Springer.

As for writing and publishing, this is an area I could see expanding. I hope this is just the first book I will write. A work of fiction might be nice to try, but if that proves too challenging, I can always rely on the truth. I've met enough colorful characters in my life as a traveling musician and within my own family that I'd be busy for quite a while before that well would dry up.

Even before 2009, Steve Richard and Chris Pauley of Curve Productions and I began writing a screenplay for a movie called *Now*. It's a completely fictional story inspired by the song I've included with this book. We'd like to finish that screenplay, find some funding, and make the film. If that happens, there may be an opportunity for me to expand my limited acting experience in the process, but any future contract will insist that I be joined by three men in silly costumes in any scene I do . . . love scenes excluded.

Songwriting now holds even more promise than ever, with so many doors opening to me in the traditional sense, but also with companies and individuals who see the value in investing in a song for themselves. It is an awesome challenge and very rewarding to take on single-song projects for others, whether they are companies wanting a meaningful tribute to the essence of what they do well, or individuals who simply want a family member's life immortalized in a song (like my grandmother's "God Save Doreen").

So I'll leave this story as I began it: as a songwriter trying to make a positive difference in the world with his music. I'll also leave as a musician transformed through an experience that taught me that all of us have a powerful voice, and that our voices are worthy of being heard.

I hope you've been entertained by my experience, but if this book could impress just one thing upon you,

I would want it to be the conviction that we all have the ability to accomplish great things, especially in the age of social media. By realizing and focusing on the commonalities we share with every other person on the planet, we have the ability to energize a vast network of connections to improve the world. Most of all, when caring is at the center of our intention, our potential is truly unlimited.

Since the release of "United Breaks Guitars," everything about my life has changed, and I've traveled the world doing things I've never done before. But most people are unaware of the most significant impact of all, personally speaking. Because I was planning on giving up on the music business at the time of the video's launch, the biggest fallout of "United Breaks Guitars" is that I still have a music career!

I've often joked that "United broke my career and broke it wide open!" In 2009, I was on a waiting list for a firefighting job that I was told was coming. It took longer than expected, and it was just after the second anniversary of the launch of "UBG" that the Halifax fire department called and offered me a position. I took a week to discuss it with my friends and family and consider all the advantages that come with being a firefighter: the stability, certainty, pension, and not having to travel. But in light of all that has happened and the opportunities before me, I respectfully declined.

I've decided that I am first and foremost a singer-songwriter and that pursuing my dreams of making a difference with my music is still my life's passion. There's no telling how long I can sustain this, but I have faith in myself, and I am certainly doing it at present. For now, that's enough.

For my son, Flynn, I'd like him to know the value in chasing down his own dreams, especially in the face of uncertainty, and I've discovered that the best teachers teach by example. If I wasn't already committed, I'm in with both feet now, and I know firsthand from this whole experience . . . everything is possible.

♫ ♪ ♫ ♪ ♫

LYRICS

Please visit **www.davecarrollspecial.com/free**
to get free MP3 downloads of the six songs listed here.

(All words and music by Dave Carroll, except where noted.)

"UNITED BREAKS GUITARS"

I flew United Airlines on my way to Nebraska.
The plane departed Halifax connecting in Chicago's O'Hare.
While on the ground a passenger said from the seat behind me,
"My God, they're throwing guitars out there!"

The band and I exchanged a look, best described as terror,
From the action on the tarmac and knowing whose projectiles these would be.
So before I left Chicago I alerted three employees,
Who showed complete indifference towards me.

Chorus:
United, United,
You broke my Taylor guitar.
United, United,
Some big help you are.
You broke it, you should fix it,
You're liable, just admit it.
I should have flown with someone else or gone by car,
'Cause "United Breaks Guitars."

When we landed in Nebraska, I confirmed what I'd suspected.
My Taylor'd been the victim of a vicious act of malice at O'Hare.
And so began a yearlong saga of pass the buck, "don't ask me,"
And "I'm sorry, sir, your claim can go nowhere."

So to all the airline's people (from New York to New Delhi),
Including kind Ms. Irlweg, who says the final word from them is No.
I've heard all your excuses, and I've chased your wild gooses,
And this attitude of yours, I say, must go.

Chorus

Bridge:
Well, I won't say that I'll never fly with you again,
'Cause maybe, to save the world I probably would,
But that won't likely happen,
And if it did I wouldn't bring my luggage,
'Cause you'd just go and break it,
Into a thousand pieces,
Just like you broke my heart.
When "United Breaks Guitars."

Chorus

"UNITED BREAKS GUITARS: SONG TWO"

What did you mean when you said you were sorry?
I'm a bit confused.
I think you owe for wrecking my guitar.
But you don't think you do.
I found a guy to fix it for 1,200 bucks,
But you tell me that you're sorry and it's my tough luck.
United sees no need to make anything right.
Oh, Ms. Irlweg, we don't need to fight.

Chorus:
If you'd just come to your senses,
Accept the consequences, of you letting certain baggage handlers
Smash my property.
We could be best buddies, but our friendship has been muddied
By a flawed United Airlines policy.

I sense a tone in your last couple e-mails,
Why is that the case?
Is it that I've got questions, you've got the answers
You don't wanna face?
You've gone dark and silent as a submarine,
Leavin' me hangin' like *Apollo 13,*
Adrift in space, with no end in sight.
Oh, Ms. Irlweg, we don't need to fight.

Chorus
Tuba solo
Chorus

"UNITED BREAKS GUITARS: SONG THREE"

I had some trouble with United.
I wrote a song and put it on YouTube,
And it went around the world,
From Timmins to Timbuktu.

Now I'm done being mad at United.
Essentially they broke my career.
I was given two new Taylors
And a heck of an interesting year.

But there's a long line of people with a story like mine
Who tell me in an e-mail every day
That United needs to change in a big way.

Chorus:
Because they're mad. (We're mad.)
I told you they were mad.
They flew United, now they're sayin': "Wish I never had."
You say that you're changin', and I hope you do,
'Cause if you don't, then who'd fly with you?

They boast about our luggage at United,
Sayin' 99-point-sumpin' don't get broke.
There's a lotta bags'll make it, but a heck of a bunch that won't.

Now they're not all bad apples at United.
Some of them are only slightly bruised.
But we've all known some bad ones, as shown in those millions of views.

So now I've come to face that some time or place,
We'll be begging them in vain to right a wrong.
And we're out of patience, and I'm out of songs.

Chorus

Bridge:
United needs to understand, their customers ain't helpless.
And while they sit and ponder that, let's hear from Jerry Douglas.

Dobro solo
Chorus

"GOD SAVE DOREEN"

(chorus lyrics and melody adapted from "God Save the Queen")

Doreen Lucy Tugwood started breathing
September 1, 1922,
In a place called Romney Marsh,
In a little part of England, known to few.

Her canvas started out as plain as any.
But a steady hand with paint so rich in love,
Produced a masterpiece framed by family and faith in God above.

Chorus:
Send her victorious, happy, and glorious,
Long to reign over us,
God save our Queen.

Doreen Lucy Carroll, she got married
To a soldier sent to fight a world war.
She sailed in secret convoy to his home in Canada in '44.

She landed safe in Halifax, a stranger,
Just 21 with a daughter and a son.
They took a train to Arnprior and waited for the war to be done.

Chorus

Bridge:
And she met her share of obstacles with stoic English grace.
Two husbands and a daughter have been readying a place.
And when the good Lord calls her, we won't question where she goes.
We'll know, we'll know, we'll know, we'll know.

Doreen Lucy Daley has been painting,
Living nearly four score years and ten.
A mother, wife, and friend,
A loyal Christian Englishwoman to the end.

There are those who measure life in dollars,
But Doreen knows it's love you leave behind.
On her family tree her love abounds,
In her 25 new lines.

Chorus:
Send her victorious, happy, and glorious,
Long to reign over us,
God save our Queen.
God save Doreen.

"EVERYDAY HEROES"

Firefighters at the station listen as the tone goes out.
Fire alarms activated, and building is showing smoke,
And so the engine rolls to trouble again.
There's people at the scene just watchin'
People running out for their lives.
The firefighters get there and help them out,
And go looking for more inside,
'Cause that's just what they do, these women and men.

Chorus:
'Cause they made a promise and here they come.
Someone hurtin' called 911.
And the siren's saying hope is on the way.
There's a hero racing to help a stranger today.

Saturday night in the city, the cruiser gets a dispatched call.
A little girl says her daddy's mad,
And drank a bunch of alcohol.
And so they head away, into trouble again.
The people at the house are screaming,
And someone yells, "He's got a gun!"
A little girl full of panic cries out,
"Daddy, don't you shoot my mom,"
And that's where the cops come in,
These women and men.

Chorus

Bridge:
When people in the world need savin'
The saviors who answer the call,
Don't get paid any more for danger,
Or get to pick the ones they want.

They just go to where the few will go,
To maybe lay it all on the line.
As they do their job, and do it one more time.

Chorus

"NOW"

When there's no way out, there's still a way through.
So don't give up whatever you do.
Surrender to moments and things as they are.
From the gaps in your catch-22's.
When there's no way out, there's still a way through.

Chorus:
'Cause Now's all there is,
So peaceful and still,
In Now you don't worry 'bout what's happened or what will.
'Cause Now never ends,
And Now's never been,
And all of your answers are waiting for you here Now.

When your world stands tough and weighin' you down,
And you've had enough of this merry-go-round,
End your resistance to walls you won't move

And runnin' through old déjà vu's.
When there's no way out, there's still a way through.

Chorus

Bridge:
And when you don't understand,
How things got so far away from all you planned,
And your life, it feels so hard,
In your fragile house of cards,
Turn to your cornerstone when you're tired and feel alone,
To find your way through.

Chorus

♬ ♪ ♬ ♪ ♬

ACKNOWLEDGMENTS

This book came about through the introduction of "United Breaks Guitars" to Wayne Dyer via his daughter Tracy, who operates **UrbanJunket.com**. I am eternally grateful for the opportunity. I am also extremely grateful to Hay House CEO Reid Tracy for having faith in an untested writer, and to his assistant, Stacey Smith, for never replying to my e-mails with the words "You again?" Thanks to Leon Nacson, also with Hay House, for the work we will do in Australia, and to Alex Freemon for overseeing the final edit. And of course, special thanks to Louise Hay for creating Hay House and giving my story a home.

I have been extremely fortunate to be surrounded by so many people who have believed in me and my goings-on before and since "United Breaks Guitars." This list represents the tip of the iceberg, though, since the millions of people who tuned in and told their friends to watch "UBG" are responsible for my success. Thank you all.

Thank you to my wife, Jill, for her unwavering support and insight; my mom and dad for everything moms and dads do; and my brother, Don, for rooting for me in my good fortune. Other people who have gone beyond family, friendship, and the call of duty include: my grandmother Doreen Daley; my father-in-law, Brent Sansom; Janice Garden; Debbie, Wayne, and Brennah Pennell; Steve Stewart and the girls; Johanna Harrison;

Julian Marentette; Scott Ferguson; Lara Cassidy; Steve Richard; Chris Pauley; Barb Richard; Joshua Young; Todd Murchie; Jimmy Inch; Chris Iannetti; Mike Hiltz; Christine Buiteman; Phil Salterio; Charlie Palmer; Karen Murdoch; Paula Robbins; Jamie Robinson; Jerry Douglas; Ray Legere; Kim Dunn; Jamie Gatti; Ian Sherwood; Ross Pierce; Tom McLellan Music; Ryan Moore; Chief Steve Comeau; Halifax Regional Fire & Emergency; MacFarlands rentals; Music Nova Scotia; Rob McGee; Brent Combs; Neal Alderson; Alyson Queen; Phil Holmes; Ian Cavanagh; Hugh Bray; Tim Hardy; Mike Campbell; Mickey Quase; George Heinrichs; Paul Sparkes; Mike Havard; Harland Suttis; Bob Taylor; Chalise Zolezzi; Robin Urbanski; David Meerman Scott; Chip Bell; Jeffrey Joffey; Frank McKenna; Jeffrey Gitomer; Keith Pearce; Lara Booth; Jason Mittelstaedt; Pierre Belanger; Judea Cassyn; Dr. Fronie Leroy; all of the extras in "UBG2" and "UBG3"; Gene Simmons; Whoopi Goldberg; and Ms. Irlweg.

Special thanks to Josh Bernoff for his support, advice, and editorial contribution; and to the universe for introducing me to Simone Graham when I needed a dedicated editor.

♬ ♪ ♬ ♪ ♬

ABOUT THE AUTHOR

Dave Carroll is a singer-songwriter and social-media innovator from Halifax, Canada. Following his 2009 YouTube music-video release called "United Breaks Guitars," about his poor customer-service experience with United Airlines, Dave's career blossomed, and he is now a highly sought-after performer, content creator, author, keynote speaker, and consumer advocate.

www.davecarrollmusic.com
www.sonsofmaxwell.com
dave@davecarrollmusic.com
twitter.com/DaveCarroll
facebook.com/DaveCarrollMusic

♫ ♪ ♫ ♪ ♫

Hay House Titles of Related Interest

YOU CAN HEAL YOUR LIFE, the movie,
starring Louise L. Hay & Friends
(available as a 1-DVD program and an expanded 2-DVD set)
Watch the trailer at: **www.LouiseHayMovie.com**

THE SHIFT, the movie,
starring Dr. Wayne W. Dyer
(available as a 1-DVD program and an expanded 2-DVD set)
Watch the trailer at: **www.DyerMovie.com**

♫ ♫ ♫

BRAND NEW YOU: Reinventing Work, Life & Self Through the Power of Personal Branding, by Simon Middleton

FROM THE REARVIEW MIRROR: Reflecting on Connecting the Dots, by Bill Milliken

THE GIFT OF FIRE: How I Made Adversity Work for Me, by Dan Caro, with Steve Erwin

INSPIRED DESTINY: Living a Fulfilling and Purposeful Life, by Dr. John F. Demartini

THE MINDFUL MANIFESTO: How Doing Less and Noticing More Can Help Us Thrive in a Stressed-Out World, by Dr. Jonty Heaversedge & Ed Halliwell

WISHES FULFILLED: Mastering the Art of Manifesting, by Dr. Wayne W. Dyer

All of the above are available at your local bookstore, or may be ordered by contacting Hay House (see next page).

♫ ♫ ♫

We hope you enjoyed this Hay House book. If you'd like to receive our online catalog featuring additional information on Hay House books and products, or if you'd like to find out more about the Hay Foundation, please contact:

Hay House, Inc., P.O. Box 5100, Carlsbad, CA 92018-5100
(760) 431-7695 or (800) 654-5126
(760) 431-6948 (fax) or (800) 650-5115 (fax)
www.hayhouse.com® • www.hayfoundation.org

♫ ♫ ♫

Published and distributed in Australia by: Hay House Australia Pty. Ltd., 18/36 Ralph St., Alexandria NSW 2015 • *Phone:* 612-9669-4299 *Fax:* 612-9669-4144 • www.hayhouse.com.au

Published and distributed in the United Kingdom by: Hay House UK, Ltd., 292B Kensal Rd., London W10 5BE *Phone:* 44-20-8962-1230 • *Fax:* 44-20-8962-1239 www.hayhouse.co.uk

Published and distributed in the Republic of South Africa by: Hay House SA (Pty), Ltd., P.O. Box 990, Witkoppen 2068 *Phone/Fax:* 27-11-467-8904 • www.hayhouse.co.za

Published in India by: Hay House Publishers India, Muskaan Complex, Plot No. 3, B-2, Vasant Kunj, New Delhi 110 070 *Phone:* 91-11-4176-1620 • *Fax:* 91-11-4176-1630 www.hayhouse.co.in

Distributed in Canada by: Raincoast, 9050 Shaughnessy St., Vancouver, B.C. V6P 6E5 • *Phone:* (604) 323-7100 *Fax:* (604) 323-2600 • www.raincoast.com

♫ ♫ ♫